CU00663346

The Resource Curse

The Economy | Key Ideas

These short primers introduce students to the core concepts, theories and models, both new and established, heterodox and mainstream, contested and accepted, used by economists and political economists to understand and explain the workings of the economy.

Published

Behavioural Economics
Graham Mallard

Degrowth
Giorgos Kallis

The Living Wage
Donald Hirsch and Laura Valadez-Martinez

Marginalism
Bert Mosselmans

The Resource Curse
Syed Mansoob Murshed

The Resource Curse

Syed Mansoob Murshed

agenda
publishing

To my son, Zac Mohib

© Syed Mansoob Murshed 2018

This book is copyright under the Berne Convention.
No reproduction without permission.
All rights reserved.

First published in 2018 by Agenda Publishing

Agenda Publishing Limited
The Core
Bath Lane
Newcastle Helix
Newcastle upon Tyne
NE4 5TF
www.agendapub.com

ISBN 978-1-911116-48-6 (hardcover)
ISBN 978-1-911116-49-3 (paperback)

British Library Cataloguing-in-Publication Data
A catalogue record for this book is available from the British Library

Typeset by Out of House Publishing
Printed and bound in the UK by TJ International

Contents

Acknowledgements

I would like to thank Alison Howson of Agenda for encouraging me to write this book. My thanks also go to an anonymous reviewer, as well as Elissaios Papyrakis and Lorenzo Pellegrini of the ISS in the Hague for comments on the initial draft. Muhammad Badiuzzaman is thanked for helping to format the text, obtain data for several of the tables and charts and prepare the index. Last, but not the least, my loving gratitude goes to my seven-year-old son Zac, who cheerfully put up with his father working on the book at all hours and at weekends. It is only right and proper that this work is lovingly dedicated to him.

1

Introduction: explaining the resource curse

How could nature's bounty turn into a curse? It strains credulity to think that environmental gifts such as land, water, forests, minerals and fuels could become a curse for nations or peoples richly endowed with them. Yet the term "resource" or "natural resource curse" (see Auty 1993 for an early use of the expression) has gained currency in the last quarter of a century among economists and social scientists. Some have argued that the scepticism with which natural resource endowments are viewed harks back to Adam Smith (see Lederman & Maloney 2007).[1] It refers to the stylized fact that developing countries richly endowed with, or heavily dependent on, natural-resource-based economic activities on the whole consistently underperform compared to resource-"poor" developing countries. Among the many examples cited to support this claim are comparisons between resource-poor countries in East Asia, such as South Korea, and oil-rich African or Latin American states, such as Nigeria or Venezuela. Economies in the latter group performed poorly in the last quarter of the twentieth century.

Is this poor performance due to the countries' natural resource status? The 1980s and 1990s were lost decades for sub-Saharan African economies, as were the 1980s for the Latin American region (see Table 1.1), and, therefore, other regional or neighbourhood factors could also be at work. Table 1.1 shows that more recently, after 2000, developing country growth was robust in nearly all regions and countries, and there was also a commodity price boom that has just ended. Thus, evidence for the deleterious economic effects of the resource curse may have become weaker.

---

1. Although Smith (1976 [1776]), like many classical economists, viewed land as a factor constraining the growth of output; hence an increase in available land relaxed that constraint.

Table 1.1 GDP per capita growth rates (annual average %)

Area/country	1960–1970	1970–1980	1980–1990	1990–2000	2000–2010
All developing countries	3.1	3.3	1.2	1.9	5.2
East Asia and Pacific	2.9	4.5	5.9	6.0	8.2
Latin America and Caribbean	2.6	3.4	−0.8	1.7	1.9
Middle East and North Africa	–	–	0.5	1.7	3.1
South Asia	1.8	0.7	3.5	3.2	5.2
Sub-Saharan Africa	2.6	0.8	−1.1	−0.4	3.1

Sources: Murshed (2008) for the 1960–2000 periods (at 1995 constant US dollars) and author's own estimation for the 2001–10 period (at 2010 constant US dollars), based on data in World Bank (2015).

The economic misfortunes that beset resource-rich developing economies in contrast to their relatively resource-poor counterparts appears to be a phenomenon that began to be highlighted during the latter part of the twentieth century, particularly during the last two decades. This is, in no small degree, attributable to the extraordinary economic success achieved by certain resource-poor East Asian countries such as South Korea, whose average standard of living has caught up with richer industrialized countries, in contrast to the relative decline in resource-rich Latin America and Africa. Hence, it could be contended that the resource curse played a part in the economic reversal of fortunes between countries in East Asia and sub-Saharan Africa between 1960 and the present time. In 1960 sub-Saharan African countries were, on average, richer than East Asian countries, whereas that position had been reversed by the end of the twentieth century. Acemoglu, Johnson and Robinson (2002) employ the expression "reversal of fortune" to describe long-term growth patterns leading to a reversal of the relative prosperity of countries nearer the equator compared to countries in the temperate zone between the year 1500 and the present. In *c.* 1500 nations closer to the equator in Asia, such as China, were believed to be more affluent than countries located to the North.

Before the end of the twentieth century there was scant discussion of a resource curse.[2] True, Prebisch (1950) and Singer (1950) spoke of a long-term trend of declining commodity prices relative to the price of manufacturing because of the low income inelasticity of demand for primary commodities.[3] Their pessimism about commodity prices was, in no small degree, driven by the interwar experience and the Great Depression of the 1930s, when commodity prices collapsed. Be that as it may, this elasticity pessimism led many to advocate a growth strategy based on (manufacturing) import substitution to build up domestic industrial strength. This was gradually replaced by faith in a more outward-oriented export-led growth strategy in the 1980s.

Findlay and Lundahl (1999) present evidence on the economic performance of natural-resource-rich countries in the 1870–1914 period, an epoch that has come to be known as the first era of globalization, driven by a huge surge in international trade and investment. They contend that this was a period of high growth for resource-abundant nations, driven by high demand for natural-resource-based products in the industrialized parts of Europe, manifesting itself in the huge expansion in international trade in terms of both volume and value.[4] This is a time when factor endowments and the principle of comparative advantage dictated that resource-rich nations exported primary goods in return for the manufactures supplied by industrialized nations.

In the regions of recent settlement[5] the abundance of natural resources created linkages to manufacturing, but this effect is either absent or less effective elsewhere. Findlay and Lundahl (1999) point out the need to distinguish between the experience of the regions of recent settlement and

---

2. Economic historians, however, point out that a type of resource curse was at work in Imperial Spain in the sixteenth to eighteenth centuries as a result of the country's seizure of silver and precious metals from Latin America; see Drelichman (2005).

3. This argument is mainly applicable to unprocessed primary commodities, but need not apply to many processed natural resource goods that are turned into "niche" products, such as fragrant rice, New World wine or Pacific salmon.

4. Prebisch had pointed out that technical progress in manufacturing would lead to a higher demand for primary commodities, pushing up their prices. In short, growth in manufacturing-based economies would drive "world" growth.

5. A term used to characterize countries in the "New" World settled by Europeans who became a majority in those countries, such as in the United States, Canada, Australia and New Zealand.

the "tropics". Within the "tropical" category, a further distinction could be made between mineral producers (Bolivia, Chile, South Africa, for example), mixed primary commodity producers (Colombia, Costa Rica, Ceylon, Malaya), large plantation agricultural countries (Brazil, Argentina) and peasant or smallholder agricultural economies (Burma, Siam). A mixed picture of economic progress and structural transformation between 1870 and 1914 appears for the various "tropical economies". The most salient characteristic driving growth and real wages was the presence of surplus labour, as in densely populated countries such as China and India. Growth in commodity-exporting nations collapsed during the Great Depression as a result of the interwar trade collapse, leading to the Prebisch–Singer position gaining credence in the early post-1950 era.

Myint (1958) argued that in sparsely populated developing countries the expansion in international trade during the first era of economic globalization (1870–1914) provided a vent for surplus[6] for underutilized capacity, leading to institutional change and enhanced growth. He had in mind the examples of the rice-producing[7] peasant economies of his native Burma, and Thailand, in the nineteenth century.

There may, however, be the danger of excessive dependence of the economy on a staple product,[8] but not if the economy is adaptable to change and able to switch to new staples, as in the case of Canada (from fur to cod, and so on). This has led to its adaptation, more contemporaneously, by Auty (2007) as the staple "trap", a term used to characterize an economy that is unable to transform its economy to produce and depend on newer products and economic activities. Later, we shall see the importance of distinguishing an *abundance* of natural resources, in economies such as in the United States, from excessive *dependence* on crude natural-resource-based exports (Brunnschweiler & Bulte 2008).

The aim of this book is to trace a common thread that runs through the various strands of the resource curse thesis, as it relates to contemporary economics, covering various aspects of the curse at both the theoretical and empirical levels. A greater reliance on natural-resource-based products

6. An expression attributed to Adam Smith in his *Wealth of Nations* (1976 [1776]).
7. In Burma (Myanmar) and Thailand (Siam) total rice production was in surplus to domestic demand, unlike in most parts of South Asia.
8. As pointed out by Canadian economic historian Harold Innis (1930).

is said to bring about risks in resource misallocation, the wrong kinds of specialization, poorer growth rates, rent-seeking, inferior governance, less democracy and enhanced possibilities of civil war. If this is the case, we need to examine the theoretical mechanisms underlying the curse, which receive less attention nowadays compared to empirical evidence. I will attempt a review of the (now voluminous) empirical evidence on the resource curse – something that is becoming increasingly technically sophisticated, yet still yields only mixed results. Recent surveys of the empirical resource curse literature include Deacon (2011), Frankel (2012), Venables (2016), Gilberthorpe and Papyrakis (2017), van der Ploeg and Poelhekke (2017) and Badeeb, Lean and Clark (2017).

Today the resource curse is associated with boom-and-bust economic growth cycles, overconsumption during booms, resource misallocation, poorer growth rates and inferior institutions of governance. Some label this as the "paradox of plenty" (Karl 1999). The contestation over natural resource rents has also been argued to be a prime cause of civil war in developing countries, with Collier and Hoeffler (2004) as its principal proponents.

At the very outset, it is helpful to get a clearer idea of the definition of the natural resources that we have in mind. The term "natural resources" implies the bounty of nature, encompassing agricultural land, water resources, fisheries and forests, as well as minerals and fuels. Of these, minerals and fuels are non-renewable and involve extraction. These resources, such as oil, gas and mineral deposits, have a tendency to lead to production and revenue patterns that are concentrated, while revenue flows from other types of resources, such as agriculture, are more diffused throughout the economy. Following the classification proposed in Auty (1997), countries rich in the former category of resource may be called "point-sourced" economies, while nations abundant in the latter type may be referred to as "diffuse". This classification is now widely accepted in the resource curse literature. The resource curse of recent years mainly applies to economies in developing countries heavily reliant on these categories of non-renewable or point-sourced natural resources. Occasionally, agricultural commodities such as coffee or cocoa are also considered point-sourced, because they are produced in plantations or marketed by monopolies in a manner that makes them akin to the concentrated conditions prevalent with minerals.

Evidence for the negative aspects of the resource curse at work was at its peak around the year 2000. Table 1.2 presents a list of 42 developing countries that are growth failures. Growth failure is defined as a country having a real per capita income level in 1998 that it had achieved much earlier (prior to 1960, or during the 1960s, or during the 1970s or during the 1980s). So, for example, the first column in Table 1.2 lists countries whose 1998 per-capita income was achieved in 1960 or earlier, the second column names countries whose 1998 per capita income was achieved during the

Table 1.2 Countries with growth failure

Catastrophic		Severe	
1960 or before	**During 1960s**	**During 1970s**	**During 1980s**
Central African Republic	Côte d'Ivoire	Burundi	Kenya
Chad	Mauritania	Cameroon	Republic of Congo
Democratic Republic of Congo[3]	Togo	Gabon	
Ghana		Malawi	Ecuador
Liberia	Bolivia	Mali	Paraguay
Madagascar	Jamaica	Zimbabwe	Trinidad and Tobago
Niger			
Nigeria[1]		El Salvador	Jordan
Rwanda		Guatemala	
Senegal		Guyana	
Sierra Leone		Honduras	
Somalia		Peru	
		Algeria[1]	
Haiti		Iran[2]	
Nicaragua		Saudi Arabia	
Venezuela			
		Philippines[1]	

Notes: Based on a sample of 98 countries for which data is available; see Perälä (2000).

[1] Economy considered large; 1960 population clearly above 25 million.

[2] Economy considered large; 1960 population clearly above 20 million.

[3] Economy considered large; 1960 population clearly above 15 million.

Sources: The World Bank's World Development Indicators tables, available at http://wdi.worldbank.org/tables (accessed 15 December 2017); and the United Nations Development Programme (UNDP 1996).

1960s, and so on. In short, the countries in Table 1.2 have all experienced negative growth over a long period.

Catastrophic growth failure is considered to have occurred in economies that attained their 1998 real per capita income level sometime during the 1960s or before. Severe growth failure, in turn, is considered to have occurred in those countries that have had more than a decade of stagnation, achieving their 1998 real per capita income level either during 1970s or 1980s. All but six of these countries can be described as having point-sourced or mineral/fuel natural resource endowments, as measured by their principal exports. The diffuse economies are Honduras, Mali, the Philippines, Senegal, Somalia and Zimbabwe. Table 1.2 is constructed on the basis of data availability on growth rates extending back to 1960 and earlier for a total of 98 countries. If we look into the picture after 1965, we could add, *at least*, Angola, Iraq and Ethiopia to the list of growth failures, based on negative growth.

More importantly, only six (or seven, if we include Oman) mineral- or fuel-exporting, point-sourced economies have real per capita income growth rates that exceeded 2.5 per cent per annum on average in the 1965–99 period; see Murshed (2004). These are Botswana, Chile, the Dominican Republic, Indonesia, Egypt and Tunisia. Of these, only two – Botswana and Indonesia – have high growth rates of over 4 per cent. We may wish to consider Malaysia as point-sourced as well. Therefore, in the developing world we had three point-sourced success stories around the year 2000, and we seemed to have an empirical prima facie case for a resource curse.

The situation looks different after 2000: both resource-rich and resource-poor countries grew successfully (Table 1.1), and growth rates in resource-rich nations caught up with resource-poor economies (Venables 2016). That situation may be changing again, however, after the petering out of the recent commodity price boom. But the dependence on natural-resource-based staples seems to persist, in terms of countries depending on extractable resources as a major revenue source (fiscal dependence), as well as export dependence. In 2012 the International Monetary Fund (IMF 2012; see also Venables 2016) classified 51 countries as resource-rich. The definition was based on these countries obtaining at least 20 per cent of their exports, and 20 per cent of their tax revenue, from non-renewable resources.

Hence the term "resource-dependent" would fit these two stylized facts better than "resource-rich".[9]

In a nutshell, the resource curse works by distorting economic signals that are harmful for the economy and its growth prospects. It is also argued to have negative effects on political institutions and channels of governance by encouraging more rent-seeking behaviour. Equally, the converse is true. It is argued that there will be no resource curse when good institutions are already present, and are resilient to the nefarious influence, if any, of resource rents, as is so often cited to be the case for oil-rich Norway (Mehlum, Moene & Torvik 2006). An abundance of natural resources also led to the widely believed claim that it was a major cause of civil war (Collier & Hoeffler 2004). Thus, there is both an economic and a political (institutional) resource curse. The politics and the economics are inseparably connected, however, and this is what I shall attempt to emphasize in the following text.

Structure of the book

I begin in Chapter 2 by examining the "Dutch disease" mechanisms by which large transfers (including a booming natural-resource-based sector) cause real exchange appreciation and rising relative prices of non-tradable *vis-à-vis* tradable goods prices. This interferes with efficiency of allocation and changes the composition of output away from the traditional exports of agricultural or manufactured goods. To put it simply, the economy bets on the wrong horse, which will, in any case, not win in the long run. These countries may miss out on the stimulus and structural transformation engendered by labour-intensive, manufactured-export-led growth (Sachs & Warner 1995, 1999a), which is said to have occurred in East Asian high-growth economies. It may even cause a permanent loss of competitiveness in manufacturing (Krugman 1987; Matsuyama 1992) and premature deindustrialization (Rodrik 2016).

In Chapter 3, I examine the institutional resource curse, and link it to economic growth failure. Acemoglu, Johnson and Robinson (2001) have

---

9. In a subset of these countries, extreme resource dependence is to be found: in 25 of these nations these commodities accounted for more than 75 per cent of exports, and in 20 countries extractable resource-based royalties and rents made up more than a half of government revenue.

succeeded in establishing the nexus between growth in the long run and good-quality institutions. Here institutions can mean the polity, such as the degree of democratic development, as well as the institutions of governance, such as the rule of law, bureaucratic quality and the control of corruption. It is noteworthy that oil dependence, in particular, is said to have retarded democratic development (Ross 2001). In addition, there is an important distinction between how natural resource booms can lead to less effective governance and the fact that the resource curse may not materialize under conditions of resilient good governance. My argument is that the best mechanism to explore to test the presence of the resource curse is to proceed by examining the effect of resource dependence on institutional quality, and then gauge how these changed institutions impact on economic performance. This is also in line with my contention that politics and economics are *inseparable*.

Chapter 4 examines the voluminous body of cross-country, mainly econometric, empirical evidence on the resource curse and growth, and on the impact of resource rents on institutions.[10] I will also consider subnational studies on the effect of resource rents, as well as some country case studies. The cross-country econometric literature gives very variable and inconclusive results as to the existence and operation of the resource curse.

In Chapter 5 I examine the "greed" motive for civil war – the situation in which the contest for natural resource rents escalates into outright civil war – and the empirical evidence for this contention. The greed motivation is losing ground to its rival paradigm, based on grievances, but, importantly, resource rents at the local level of their extraction can foment grievances leading to civil war or violence. In the ultimate analysis, the greed and grievance explanations for the onset of civil war and other types of civil conflict in developing countries are inextricably intertwined.

Chapter 6 is concerned with measures and mechanisms to manage resource rents optimally so that the economy and economic growth are sustainable. This implies leaving the total stock of wealth intact into future periods, both within and between generations. Natural resource rents are an asset, part of the total capital stock, and, when these take the form of non-renewable resources, offsetting savings and investment are necessary

---

10. Papyrakis (2017) states that the number of academic papers in a Google search on the resource curse yielded 13 results in 1995, rising to 543 by 2005 and to 2,360 by 2015!

to maintain a constant total stock of wealth, such that economic growth is sustainable and inter-generational equity is ensured. In this connection the most widely mooted mechanism is the trust fund or sovereign wealth fund, such that genuine savings (because of resource or asset depletion) are non-negative and inter-generational considerations are taken into account. Sometimes, though, a low-income developing country may optimally consume and invest some of these resource rents in the domestic economy or pay off international debt, paying less attention to future generations, who are likely to be more affluent. Finally, Chapter 7 offers some conclusions, with an attempt to link the various aspects of the resource curse literature, and a brief summary of the new directions that research into the resource curse is taking.

2

The Dutch disease and deindustrialization

This chapter explores the theory behind the resource curse thesis. It will show how the discovery of natural resources, or an increase in the demand or price of existing resources, can lead to increased rents or revenues that effectively crowd out other productive activities in the economy. A natural-resource-based revenue boom for an economy is akin to a gift, or "manna from heaven". This naturally leads to a spending boom, but also to a resource reallocation effect, in which the economy's output switches from traded goods to non-traded goods and services such as housing. This phenomenon has come to be known as the "Dutch disease".[1]

To show how this occurs, I first present a model – which is a simplified version of the Findlay and Lundahl (1994) historical "Christopher Columbus" model – inspired by the experiences of the regions of recent settlement between c. 1870 and 1914, where increases in demand for natural-resource-based products, agricultural and mineral, did not necessarily preclude growth in manufacturing. I then present my own open economy multisectoral model of the "Dutch disease" (Murshed 2001), mainly in connection with mineral and fuel price spikes, in which the syndrome can be avoided by judicious policy choices. Finally, we come to the long-term aspect of prolonged Dutch disease, namely a loss of competitiveness in manufactures, which – if not "treated" – causes permanent and premature deindustrialization.

A resource boom tends to crowd out the other leading sector of the economy. So, in countries that previously exported manufactured goods, that sector contracts (as was the case in the United Kingdom after the

---

1. An expression first used in *The Economist* in 1977. This is because the discovery of gas in the North Sea was said to have contributed to deindustrialization in the Netherlands.

discovery of North Sea oil in the 1970s, for example); in developing countries, it could be the agricultural sector. In an open economy a substantial current account surplus emerges, leading to currency appreciation under a regime of flexible exchange rates. This makes existing (non-resource-boom) exports uncompetitive in world markets. This has been argued to have contributed to the deindustrialization of the United Kingdom in the 1980s and later. It can also produce episodes of unemployment despite the oil revenue bounty, as in the United Kingdom during the early 1980s, if the exchange rate appreciates excessively (overshoots its long-run equilibrium level); see the models analysed in Murshed (1997: chap. 6). Under fixed exchange rates the price of non-traded domestically produced goods and services increases, encouraging their supply more than for traded goods that are now imported; the domestic supply of traded goods declines as more of these are imported. Either way, there is real exchange rate appreciation. There is a shift in the composition of domestic output from tradables towards non-traded goods and services.

The Christopher Columbus model

To give a simplified version of the model in Findlay and Lundahl (1994), the stylized economy is composed of two sectors: A (primary goods or unprocessed commodities, food grains, minerals, fuels, and so on); and M (manufactures, including the processing of natural-resource-based products).

The production function for the primary sector is

$$A = A(N, L) \tag{2.1}$$

where output (A) is a function of land (N) and labour (L). The most innovative feature of the model is that the endowment of "land" is not an exogenous given but can be increased by extending the frontier, as it was during the nineteenth century in many parts of the world, although chiefly in the Americas and Australasia. The process involves a cost, involving expenditure in the technology of land-clearing, requiring capital (K), with the capital devoted to this task denoted by K_A. Thus

$$K_A = f(N) \qquad (2.2)$$

In manufacturing, the production function is described as

$$M = M(K_M, L) \qquad (2.3)$$

where K_M is the capital utilized in manufacturing and L refers to labour input. In equilibrium, the marginal product of capital in manufacturing is equal to the exogenously given real interest rate (r), reflecting both the time preferences of economic agents (rate of return on saving) and the rate of return on capital.

Let P indicate the price of primary goods relative to manufactured goods prices. The supplies of N and A are a positive function of this relative price:

$$N = N(P); \; A = A(P) \qquad (2.4)$$

Globalization in the 1870–1914 period led to increased international trade and capital flows. There was a rise in the price of commodities (P) owing to the demand from industrialized countries, and an increased supply of capital (leading to a fall in r), leading to the following effects: the rise in P induces more activity in the A sector, and an extension of the land frontier, as well as greater employment in primary production. There may be a switch in the composition of output towards more primary goods production, a classic "Dutch disease" effect. A fall in r due to the greater availability of (domestic or internationally owned) capital can induce more manufacturing output, however, because a rise in manufacturing output is required to bring about the profit-maximizing marginal value product of capital equal to its now lower rate of return. If the two developments (the rise in P and the fall in r) occur simultaneously, say because there is more demand for primary products and capital is more internationally mobile, then an extension of the land frontier to produce more commodities, fuel or minerals is possible as long as any decline (due to increased production) in the profit rate on extending the land frontier is less than the fall in real interest rates (r). Thus, commodity booms do not rule out growth in manufacturing (no Dutch disease) and increases in the economy-wide real wage rate. A shortage of labour, particularly in the A sector, may induce immigration. This will not reduce the equilibrium real wage, as this is determined by labour productivity in manufacturing and the rate of return on capital (the real interest rate, r).

The experience outlined above pertains most to the regions of recent settlement inhabited by settlers from Europe. In the other parts of the world, which make up today's developing countries, the situation may be quite different. For one, there may have been no forward or backward linkages from the agricultural sector to demand for domestic manufacturing, in the manner outlined in Baldwin (1956), the absence of which is more likely in plantation or subsistence economies. Successful structural change into manufacturing growth is more likely where smallholder agriculture, as opposed to capital-intensive mining, is more prevalent; especially if it is promoted by the state through agricultural extension schemes, it can create demand for locally manufactured consumption and capital goods. Second, there may be surplus labour, leading to an exogenously given and fixed real wage – in which case there is no net increase in the real wage rate following the commodity boom and increased exports. The capital needed to clear the land may come from abroad, and the increased production of commodities may take place in plantations, employing hired labour from a population paid a fixed subsistence wage.

The Dutch disease in a multisectoral model[2]

It should be borne in mind that the effects of the "Dutch disease" on the macroeconomy represent the short to medium run; long-run effects of protracted resource booms or prolonged resource dependence are described in the next section.

In the case of a multisectoral model for the economy, there are three sectors on the real side, two of which are traded goods, and one a non-traded commodity. A monetary sector is also incorporated. The model, despite the stylization, is richer than comparable theoretical models, such as that in Sachs and Warner (1999b). The purpose of the model is not just to represent "Dutch disease" but also to contrast what was considered to be the significant difference between East Asian economies and (initially)

---

2. The material in this section is closely based on Murshed (2001). A more technical version with full derivations can be found in Murshed (1999).

higher-wage Latin American countries that failed to go through the phase of exporting labour-intensive manufactured goods.[3]

Sachs and Warner (2001) present empirical evidence suggesting that countries rich in natural resources tend to have higher price levels, and as a result their non-natural-resource-based goods are uncompetitive and cannot be exported. They therefore miss out on the benefits of export-led growth that many other developing countries poorly endowed with natural resources have gained from, say in East Asia. They also argue that a high natural resource endowment adversely affects growth even after previous growth and other factors that militate against economic growth are taken into account, such as a tropical location, distance from the sea and a high disease burden.

A multisectoral model

The first traded good in the economy is denoted by R, for the natural-resource-based sector, whose output is entirely exogenous and purely for export. R represents the value of exports from this sector in domestic currency units. The value of output in the resource-based sector is treated exogenously, following Sachs (1999), Sachs and Warner (1999a) and other treatments of "Dutch disease" models, as in Neary and van Wijnbergen (1986). R could also include foreign aid and other transfers, such as worker remittances from abroad.

M indexes the other traded sector, which is both consumed domestically and exported. It is, basically, labour-intensive manufactured goods. In addition, there are consumption imports, C_p, which compete with M in domestic consumption. M is produced utilizing labour only, following Sachs (1999), in order to capture the part played by labour-intensive manufactured goods for export and domestic consumption. The price of M (P_T) is normalized at unity, and this price is in any case given in a small open economy. Following Sachs (1999), the supply of M is described by

---

3. The experience of Africa in this context is similar to that of Latin America, because most African economies are relatively resource-rich, but with lower real wages compared to Latin America.

$$M = \theta L_M \qquad (2.5)$$

where L_M represents labour employed in the M sector and θ stands for the marginal value product of labour in that sector.

The non-traded goods sector is represented by N, the production of which requires capital, labour and an imported intermediate input (T), as in Sachs (1999). It therefore needs some foreign technological input, and is the capital-intensive sector by definition. In a sense the output of the N sector is more "sophisticated" than in the other sectors, but perhaps that is precisely why it is non-traded. Note that manufacturing could lie within either the M or the N sector, and the "real-life" counterpart of the non-traded sector is not restricted to public and private services. In summary, the output of the N sector could include government services and private services, as well as some shielded manufacturing. For the sake of analytical convenience, fixed proportions characterize the use of the intermediate input from abroad in the N sector (see Findlay & Rodriguez 1977 for a discussion of production functions when an imported input enters in this fashion). The output of the N sector can be represented as

$$P_N N = P_N N(P_N, E) \qquad (2.6)$$

where P_N represents the price of the non-tradable good. The supply of N increases with P_N but declines as the nominal exchange rate depreciates (E increases), as this makes the intermediate input more expensive. As far as the domestic value added of the N sector is concerned, this is obtained by subtracting the value of the intermediate input:

$$(P_N - \lambda)N(P_N, E) = (P^D_N)N \qquad (2.7)$$

where $\lambda = ET$, and P^D_N measures domestic value added in the N sector.

Turning to consumption, or the demand side, in the traded manufactured goods sector this is composed of domestic demand (C_M) and foreign or export demand (X_M):

$$C_M(P_N, Y, E) + X_M(E) = M \qquad (2.8)$$

Domestic demand for the output of the M sector depends positively on the price of the non-traded good, P_N, as well as income, Y. It is also positively related to the exchange rate; a rise in E represents devaluation, an increase in the cost of obtaining imported substitutes. Export demand is positively related to the nominal exchange rate. Equation (2.8), therefore, represents equilibrium in the M sector. It can be interpreted as demand, on the left-hand side, equalling supply, on the right-hand side; excess demand causes output to rise.

In the non-traded goods sector, equilibrium supply equals demand is represented by

$$C_N(P_N, Y) + I_N(r) = (P_N - \lambda)N(P_N, E) \qquad (2.9)$$

Excess demand causes the relative price of N, P_N to be bid up to restore equilibrium. Domestic consumption of non-tradables is negatively related to its own price and positively linked to income. I_N stands for investment – that is, the savings leading to capital formation in that sector, negatively related to the interest rate (r).

We need to specify the concept of national income, Y. This consists of domestic value added in all three productive sectors, N, M and R, less imports. Thus

$$Y = (P_N - \lambda)N(P_N, E) + M + R - EC_F(E, Y) \qquad (2.10)$$

It is useful at this stage to define an overall price index (P), representing the aggregate cost of consumption of all three goods: imported consumption goods (priced by E), non-traded goods and domestic non-resource-based traded goods prices. This price index is a cost of living or consumer price index. It represents the cost of purchasing a basket of goods comprising imported consumer goods, non-tradables and traded goods. The prices of the three consumption goods are represented by E, P_N and P_T respectively.[4] The consumer price index is of use in measuring the real consumption wage and arriving at an appropriate definition of real money balances. The consumer price index takes the form

---

4. The exponents in P (β, α and $1 - \alpha - \beta$) represent the weights or shares of the three goods in the representative consumers consumption basket. They sum to unity.

$$P = E^{\beta} P_N{}^{\alpha} P_T{}^{(1-\alpha-\beta)}$$

or

$$P_T = 1, P = E^{\beta} P_N{}^{\alpha} \qquad (2.11)$$

The monetary sector for this economy takes the following form:

$$H(Y, r) = H/P \qquad (2.12)$$

Equation (2.12) represents equilibrium on the monetary side of the economy. Excess demand for money will push up equilibrium interest rates. Money demand, on the left-hand side of (2.12), is negatively related to interest rates and positively linked to Y. The latter also incorporates the wealth effect of resource booms: a rise in the value of R will not only impact on goods demand but also raise asset (money) demand. H denotes the value of nominal balances. When it is deflated by the consumer price index, P, we obtain the value of real balances. Note also that changes in the exchange rate will impact on real balances; for example, nominal exchange rate depreciation or devaluation (rise in E) lowers real money supply.

Finally, we come to the balance of trade:

$$R + X_M(E) - EC_F(E, Y) - ETN(.) = F \qquad (2.13)$$

The left-hand side represents the trade balance or exports minus imports. There are two exports: the natural-resource-based exports as well as the manufactured traded sector's exports. The two imports are consumption and intermediate inputs respectively. F stands for the trade balance, which is positive if there is a trade surplus, negative if there is a deficit. I postulate a fixed exchange rate regime. This corresponds to the stylized facts for the vast majority of developing countries. Under a system of fixed exchange rates, the balance of payments is a residual in the short run, improvements in the trade balance cause an increase in the stock of foreign exchange reserves, F, and vice versa. Flexible exchange rates can be easily incorporated, however. This will add an extra endogenous variable, E, into the system. E will rise (depreciate) with balance of payments deficits, and vice versa. For the sake of tractability, I have omitted capital flows from Equation (2.13); this makes the trade balance equivalent to the balance of payments. Since the model that follows is not a growth model, I cannot meaningfully incorporate human capital. If the accumulation of human capital takes place only as a result of increased employment in the M sector, however (Sachs & Warner 1999a), we can say that an increase in the output of M increases the stock of human capital.

It ought to be emphasized at this juncture that the distinction between point-sourced and diffuse natural-resource-based economies is similar to the Latin American and East Asian characterization contained in Sachs (1999). In Latin America, and in Africa, there is a greater tendency to rely on exports of the resource sector. In the East Asian case the more important exportable is labour-intensive manufactures.[5] Sachs (1999) also asserts that non-traded and imported consumption goods figure more largely in the Latin American consumption basket, relative to East Asia. Sachs (1999) states that in the typical East Asian economy it is M that is the labour-intensive sector, whereas it is N in Latin America.

Dutch disease phenomena occur as a result of natural resource discoveries, an increase in the world price of mineral exports, or increased transfers, captured by an exogenous increase in R in the model. The resource boom raises asset or money demand, which pushes up domestic interest rates, r, which in turn dampen investment (capital accumulation) in the N sector (see Murshed 1997: chap. 6 for details).

When we examine the combined effect of the rise in R on both the N and M sectors, four possibilities occur. First, both M and N could expand. This will happen if there is a high propensity to consume non-tradable goods, a low wealth effect of the resource boom on money demand and a low interest rate response to investment in non-traded goods. The second possibility is for the non-traded sector to expand while the traded sector M contracts – the Latin American case. This requires that the price elasticity of non-traded goods demand (C_{NI}) is low or inelastic. In other words, the rise in P_N as that sector expands does not reduce demand by very much. This is, of course the classic Dutch disease outcome. Third, there is the stylized

---

5. In East Asia, over time, higher-value-added technologically and human-capital-intensive manufactured exports have taken over from unskilled labour-intensive manufactured goods exports.

East Asian example.[6] Here it is the M sector that expands, whereas the N sector contracts. We need to have a high propensity to consume the domestically produced traded good, M. Finally, both the M and N sectors could contract. This is the most extreme form of Dutch disease, and is associated with strong wealth effects impacting on money demand.

The results above with respect to a rise in R on the N and M sectors can be depicted in terms of a diagram, in M and P_N space. In Figure 2.1 the NN and MM schedules represent equilibrium (supply equals demand) in the non-traded and traded goods markets respectively. They are both positively sloped, as an increase in either M or P_N raises income, and thus the demand for the other good goes up. The initial equilibrium in both markets occurs at the intersection point A. An upward movement in NN represents an expansionary effect on output in the N sector: NN_0 moves to NN_1. It reflects the fact that more N is demanded for each level of M. In the M sector, a rightward movement signals expansion from MM_0 to MM_1. This indicates that a greater quantity of M is demanded for each level of N produced. If the resource boom produces an expansion in both sectors, we arrive at point C in the new equilibrium following the rise in R. Contractionary effects on output are depicted by a leftward movement in the MM to MM_2, and a downward movement in NN to NN_2. If both sectors contract, point B indicates final equilibrium. The Latin American or Dutch disease outcome is shown at point E, with the non-traded sector expanding but the traded sector contracting. The diametrically opposed East Asian case is depicted at point D in Figure 2.1.

Finally, we come to the impact on the trade balance (also the balance of payments) of the resource boom. If the impact of the rise in R on total income, Y, is both positive and very large, and the propensity to import consumer goods (C_{F2}) is substantial, then there could be a reversal of initial improvements in the balance of payments. In the East Asian case, the trade balance may improve as long as C_{F2} is not very high.

Thus, the Dutch disease does not necessarily lead to a resource reallocation effect from tradables to non-tradables, or from manufacturing to services, or prevent a nascent manufacturing sector from prematurely dematerializing. There is, therefore, a role for policy to counter "Dutch

---

6.   Many Southeast Asian economies, such as Thailand and Malaysia, are resource-rich but nevertheless have substantial manufacturing. It is in Northeast Asia that truly resource-"poor" economies can be found, such as South Korea and Taiwan.

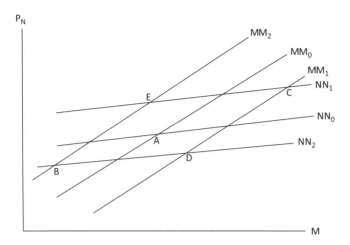

Figure 2.1 Dutch disease

disease". This can take two forms: the maintenance of international "price" competitiveness and/or domestic policies to foster industrialization.

Policy-based exchange rate depreciation (an increase in E) can be motivated by efforts to counteract Dutch disease. Devaluation, which is an increase in E, will – per (2.12) – lower the value of real money balances, and hence put upward pressure on the interest rate, r. Note that devaluation, at least upon impact, lowers the real wage as the price of imported consumption goods increases. It will also make the intermediate import more expensive in terms of domestic currency. There are two opposing effects of devaluation on imports: one is negative, on the supply side, as imported inputs cost more domestically; the other is the positive impact devaluation has by reducing consumption imports, which become more expensive in terms of the home currency. If the negative impact of devaluation on the non-traded sector is less than the positive effect of containing consumption imports, the policy will have been successful. This is more likely if consumption imports are highly price-elastic. In addition to devaluation, more directly interventionist policies could be pursued to foster the output of the tradable labour-intensive sector. One form of such policies could be an *ad valorem* tax, τ, on the price of the non-traded good, P_N. The revenues could be utilized to subsidize manufactures production; even if it contravenes World Trade Organization (WTO) rules, more WTO-compatible subsidies can be devised.

Deindustrialization

Why should the loss of competitiveness in non-natural-resource-based exports be a problem for the future? Despite exchange rate overvaluation, which renders traded goods uncompetitive in international markets, surely one might assume that competitiveness in manufactured exports can be acquired at some future date when natural resource revenues dry up? There are two problems with such a belief. The first is to do with the fact that manufactures are considered to be, far and away, the most dynamic source of growth for an economy. The reason for this is that manufacturing is believed to be both the major driver of technical progress (the ultimate reason for high growth rates), with significant backward and forward linkages with the rest of the economy, and a conduit for surplus labour (Lewis 1954) in the more densely populated developing economies.[7] Second, manufacturing competitiveness, and the market share of manufactures in the global context, is notoriously ephemeral; once lost, it is nearly impossible to regain, and many developing countries may be experiencing premature deindustrialization, as we shall see below.

There are a number of factors that can cause permanent or premature deindustrialization. The previous section highlighted the expansion in the non-traded sector. In addition to that there is an exchange rate overvaluation channel, analysed in Murshed (1997: chap. 6), which simply makes exports uncompetitive – as was the case for UK manufacturing in the 1980s.[8] But there are other mechanisms as well.

As the model in Krugman (1987) illustrates, if there are learning-by-doing effects,[9] a country whose manufacturing base is eroded during a resource boom can irreversibly lose competitiveness, even when the real exchange rate reverts to its initial level after the boom has subsided. "Learning by

---

7. Hirschman (1958) emphasizes this in the context of an economic development strategy.
8. In history, so far, no industrialized nation has experienced as much deindustrialization as the United Kingdom in terms of manufacturing value added as a proportion of national income, and the share of manufacturing employment in total employment; see Rodrik (2016) and Palma (2014).
9. Torvik (2001) also considers learning-by-doing effects in a traded, non-traded good model subjected to Dutch disease effects, which may cause output to rise or decline in both sectors, and critiques Dutch disease models that looked at learning by doing only in the traded (manufactured) sectors.

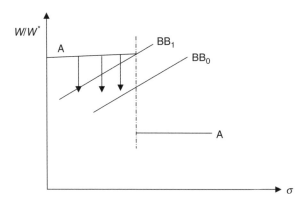

Figure 2.2 Loss of competitiveness

doing" is akin to the accumulation of capital, which renders the manufacturing sector more competitive and allows it to maintain and gain market share in the world economy. It is particularly pertinent in sectors in which innovation and research and development are important. This process of learning by doing is cumulative over time. Therefore, prolonged periods of loss of market share induce "forgetting by not doing", as the stock of knowledge capital in manufacturing diminishes. In the Krugman (1987) model depicted in Figure 2.2, the vertical axis describes the price competitiveness of the domestic sector relative to the rest of the world in terms of the relative domestic real wage ratio (W/W^*). The parameter σ gives us the number of goods in which the home country enjoys comparative advantage, whereas $1 - \sigma$ is the range of goods in which the rest of the world is competitive. The BB schedule is like a balanced trade requirement, suggesting that a higher domestic wage requires more knowledge capital to sustain manufacturing competitiveness. The AA function (knowledge capital) is like a step function with discontinuities. A temporary, but sufficiently long-lasting, upward shift of the BB line due to exchange rate appreciation (wage rises relative to productivity) will cause AA to shift down because knowledge capital is lost. Thus, temporary resource booms cause path dependence or *hysteresis*, a permanent loss of competitiveness.

For developing countries, this means that their future potential for exporting manufactured goods and diversifying the production base is stunted. If there are positive externalities from human capital accumulation in manufacturing only, as in the model developed by Matsuyama (1992), and resource booms retard the development of the more dynamic manufacturing sector, the growth path of the economy under free trade is lower than that of more resource-poor countries. The important point is that, following a boom–bust cycle associated with natural resource revenues, a country might find itself devoid of these rents, yet not industrialized and unable to catch up with other developing countries that are already moderately industrialized. Moreover, their wages may be too high to compete with other resource-poor developing nations.

In the study by Sachs and Warner (1999a), a role for growth-enhancing human capital (or skills in the work force) is incorporated into a model with a non-traded sector, a traded good and a purely exportable natural resource sector. Human capital accumulation, in the form of an externality, takes place as a result of traded/manufacturing production only. Resource booms, in the Sachs and Warner (1999a) model, retard the growth of the economy via the crowding out of production in the traded (manufactured) sector. The stock of human capital is diminished as employment in tradables declines; this in turn hampers future production of all goods, and hence the growth of the economy.

Another Sachs and Warner (1999b) paper on resource booms permits increasing returns to scale in either of the two sectors of the economy (traded or non-traded), but not in both. Increasing returns characterize the production of a range of intermediate inputs that could be employed in final production. The model then addresses whether resource booms can contribute towards "big-push"-type industrialization. A resource boom unambiguously expands the non-tradable sector, while at the same time shrinking the traded sector. If it is the expanding (non-traded) sector that uses these intermediate inputs, it may contribute to a successful big push. If the opposite is the case, and it is the traded sector that uses the intermediate inputs, big pushes are less likely. In addition, unless expectations about the future are optimistic, even the most propitious circumstances may not trigger accelerated industrialization or the big push. Implicitly, these expectations are related to the political system and social capital.

In Clarida and Findlay (1992), absolute and comparative advantage in production and international trade are endogenous and policy-induced. The mechanism via which these occur is a publicly financed knowledge-based input (non-rivalled and non-excludable) that lowers production costs, similar to the idea in Shell (1966). This input will not be provided by the private sector, and is therefore a public good. One can also think of this input as human capital, or infrastructural investment. There are two sectors in the economy, one of which is akin to a resource sector whereby the benefit from the publicly financed input in terms of lower production costs is relatively low. The other sector may be likened to manufacturing, and it derives greater benefit from the publicly provided input. Capital is sector-specific in manufacturing, whereas land is specific to the resource sector. All sectors require labour input.

In these circumstances, a resource boom will induce a lower optimal supply of the publicly financed input, as the resource sector obtains a proportionately smaller benefit from this input. Consequently, over the course of time, *both* sectors will be less productive, akin to a loss in absolute advantage in international trade. The expansion of international trade will also make countries with greater capital endowments gain absolute advantage in all sectors, as exports of manufactures increase, inducing greater provision of the cost-reducing public good. If an additional, non-traded and publicly supported consumption sector is introduced, similar to the functioning of state-owned enterprises, resource booms will retard competitiveness in both the other sectors even further in the presence of a strong societal or ruling class preference for this good. The reason is that the reduction of the supply of the publicly financed productive input is greater after a resource boom in the presence of a strong preference for a publicly supported non-traded consumption good.

Premature deindustrialization

We now turn to the phenomenon of premature deindustrialization in developing countries outside the East Asian region or late industrializers since *c.*1990 (see Rodrik 2016; Palma 2014 and the references therein). This refers to the empirical observation that countries now appear to be deindustrializing at an earlier phase of their economic development than was the case sometime earlier. This conclusion (see Rodrik 2016, for example) is arrived at when measuring a country's real per capita income when deindustrialization emerges – or, alternatively, by examining the peak or turning point in terms of when the real value-added share of manufacturing output in gross domestic product (GDP) begins to shrink, or when the share of manufacturing employment in total employment begins to decline.

It has long been accepted that in mature industrialized economies the share of manufacturing employment will decline (compared to its historical peaks in the 1950s in the United States, for example), as there is greater demand for services at higher incomes, and because of labour-saving technical progress in manufacturing. These economies have been dubbed as post-industrial societies by sociologists. But, by and large, the real value-added share of manufacturing in GDP has held its own in most industrialized (Organisation for Economic Co-operation and Development: OECD)[10] nations, despite falling employment, with the exception of the United Kingdom, where both the share of manufacturing employment in total employment and the GDP share of manufacturing real value added has declined. Figures cited in Rodrik (2016), based on Timmer, de Vries and de Vries (2014), indicate that in the United Kingdom the employment share of manufacturing fell from 33 per cent in the 1970s to about 10 per cent in 2013, whereas the real value added of manufacturing declined from about 25 per cent to less than 15 per cent at present. These developments have chiefly been attributed to labour-saving technical progress in manufacturing, the greater income elasticity of demand for services and the shift in competitive advantage in manufacturing to developing countries, especially developing Asia. It should be borne in mind, however, that the United Kingdom was the sole oil-exporting nation in the developed, early industrialized economy category, it was therefore subjected to a bout of Dutch disease that the other early industrializers did not experience.

The turning points for relative or absolute deindustrialization seem to be occurring earlier and especially for some developing countries in Africa and Latin America. Rodrik (2016) indicates that the decline in manufacturing employment share now commences at a per capita income level of US$6,000 in 1990 US dollars, with a peak share of 20 per cent of total employment for all countries on average. Manufacturing value added peaks at a much higher average income level, suggesting that relative employment in manufacturing declines earlier than the relative value derived from

---

10. This is often referred to as the grouping of rich developed countries.

manufacturing activities. In countries such as the United Kingdom, Sweden and Italy the manufacturing employment peak occurred at average incomes of US$14,000, whereas in India and many African states it is at average incomes of US$700.

Rodrik looks at patterns of deindustrialization in different global regions and finds that, within developing countries, both the share of manufacturing employment in total employment and its relative real value added in national income (GDP) has grown in Asia since 1990, a finding that is true even for resource-rich countries such as Indonesia, Malaysia and Thailand. This goes against the global trend of falling relative manufacturing employment. In Latin America and sub-Saharan Africa (excluding Mauritius) both these measures have declined, with Latin American nations experiencing the sharpest decline. Thus, middle-income and low-income regions have experienced deindustrialization much earlier compared to developed countries.

What factors underlie these developments? Developing countries, via the processes of globalization, may have imported some deindustrialization from developed countries, according to Rodrik (2016). To understand some of the underlying mechanisms, it is useful to rewrite Equation (2.5) from above with the relative price of manufacturing (P_M):

$$P_M M = \theta L_M \qquad (2.14)$$

Developing countries have also experienced growth in manufacturing labour productivity (θ), which requires fewer (unskilled) production line workers. This effect may have been more substantial in East Asia (including many of its resource-rich economies), with stronger learning-by-doing and agglomeration effects in manufacturing. At the same time all developing countries have imported the relative decline in manufacturing prices (P_M) because of total factor productivity improvements in manufacturing relative to services. Some nations, such as those in Asia, have also acquired a larger slice of manufacturing global market share because of astute industrial, commercial and exchange rate policies. Hence, for them, there has been an exogenous rise in M, akin to a positive export demand shock. Thus, both real output and employment (L_M) in manufacturing have risen in those regions. But for Latin America and Africa both these measures have declined, *despite absolute* increases in labour productivity, θ. This is because the rise in labour productivity is proportionately less than in Asia, and, for them, both P_M and M on the left-hand side of (2.14) fall on account of demand-related factors, and their smaller initial share in manufactured exports. Hence, manufacturing employment on the right-hand side of the equation must necessarily decline.

Commodity booms in recent years may have contributed to a newer form of Dutch disease, as pointed out by Palma (2014). In resource-rich countries the fall in P_M relative to commodity prices and the price of services was sharper during the boom of about a decade ago. Moreover, the failure of countervailing policies to foster industrialization causes greater deindustrialization. Most Latin American and African economies abandoned import substitution industrialization for more open (neoliberal) economic policies during the 1980s. This brought about greater structural transformation away from manufacturing in most of Latin America and in sub-Saharan economies such as South Africa and Zimbabwe, which had some manufacturing and prevented nascent manufacturing in the rest of sub-Saharan Africa from maturing.

A final note on the importance of manufacturing for a nation's economy and its political orientation is in order. Is manufacturing truly at the heart of growth, and does a percentage point manufacturing value added generate more growth in the future relative to service sector activities? Neo-Keynesians and left-leaning economists seem to think so. If so, it must be because of the externalities generated from manufacturing research and development, which lead to greater technical progress and growth. Moreover, traditionally manufacturing has absorbed the surplus labour from agriculture, allowing growth and structural change, as suggested by Lewis (1954). This has been the means through which the later industrializers of Western Europe, such as Germany, caught up with early industrializers, such as the United Kingdom. Manufacturing can also absorb unskilled labour. This is one reason why China has fared better than India in poverty reduction, as its manufacturers have absorbed more unskilled workers, whereas India's exports in information technology (IT) require more skilled labour.

As indicated, manufacturing has declined in middle- and upper middle-income Latin America, as well as in mostly low-income sub-Saharan Africa. This may have been aided by commodity price booms, and the dependence on primary goods exports in many of these countries. This may have adverse consequences for long-term growth. As pointed out by Rodrik (2016), in

Latin America there has been the growth of the informal economy, and in Africa low value-added services have accompanied greater rural-to-urban migration. The structural change to the greater contribution of services in national income is not growth-enhancing. True, high value-added services, such as finance and IT, can lead to similar productivity externalities as in manufacturing, but they are high-skill and labour-intensive, and do not absorb surplus labour.

The development of manufacturing and the formation of the industrial working class did much historically to foster greater democratization, the extension of the franchise and the emergence of the welfare state. It may have helped forge the democratic contract, discussed in Acemoglu and Robinson (2009), whereby elites engaged in redistribution to anchor their power-sharing commitment as a revolution prevention device. The decline of manufacturing may have contributed to the fraying of this democratic contract, accompanied as it has been with the retreat of the welfare state, the rise in the influence of the super-rich and the growth in income and wealth inequality since around 1980. It may have also contributed to the increase in the political influence of the alternative right in older industrialized nations, as well as the emergence of ethnic and sectarian conflict in developing countries.

This chapter has examined the theoretical mechanisms via which the Dutch disease phenomenon can negatively impact on the composition of output in the economy, with adverse effects on the traded sector of the economy. It also demonstrates that these adverse effects can be avoided by policy design. I will elaborate further on the optimal management of resource rents and windfalls in Chapter 6. I have also outlined the long-term impact of resource rents on manufacturing competitiveness, including recent developments in the global economy, which compromise manufacturing competitiveness at an earlier stage of economic development (premature deindustrialization). These make the promotion and retention of international competitiveness an even more urgent policy goal, particularly for resource-rich economies, which might otherwise slide into excessive reliance on resource-based exports, and fail to diversify their economic structures. The next question concerns how resource rents might actually harm growth prospects, and along with that have a negative impact on governance and democratic institutions. This is what we turn to in the next chapter.

3

Growth and the institutional resource curse

How do resource-rich countries end up with lower growth compared to resource-poor economies? How does the presence of significant resource rents impact negatively on political institutions (democracy) and the quality of governance? This chapter presents the theory and ideas behind the negative economic effects of the resource curse on economic growth, democracy and governance quality, such as the impact on corruption, as well as the impact of resource rents on public education spending, savings and fiscal dependence on royalties from natural resources.

We have considered the Dutch disease mechanisms that can harm the economy in the previous chapter, and it is worth noting that economies dependent on natural resource revenue rents are subject to sharp volatilities in these rents as they progress through the global boom and bust cycles in commodity prices. The best example is the case of the fluctuating price of oil in the last half a century. This volatility, in the context of an undiversified economic structure, can be a source of lower growth, as van der Ploeg and Poelhekke (2009) point out. Their finding has similarities to the implications of the celebrated Prebisch (1950) and Singer (1950) hypothesis about the secular decline in commodity prices relative to manufactured goods prices. In recent years the volatility effect may have been exacerbated by procyclical borrowing by resource-rich countries, which leaves them in a debt trap after a crash in commodity prices.

In this chapter, I begin with a sketch of the theories of economic growth, with a special focus on the long-run determinants of growth, which relies mainly on institutional explanations. The negative effects of resource rents from a political economy perspective arise when it leads to rent-seeking and corruption, which lower growth via their destructive effect on normal productive investment and hence growth. This line of reasoning is considered in the next section. Alternatively, resource rents may have a direct impact on political institutions, as well as governance; we may refer to this mechanism as the "political resource curse", discussed in the section that follows. Political institutions and the quality of governance can also impact on growth. The last section considers other potential harmful economic effects of resource rents; in this section both the mechanism and the evidence are jointly presented.

Theories of growth

A simple growth accounting exercise[1] will inform us that differences in average or per capita income between richer and poorer countries can be attributed chiefly to the former's greater capital stock (physical capital and infrastructure), as well as a superior labour force (human capital). Historically, after the "Industrial Revolution" in Britain, many nations witnessed episodes of high growth. This achievement may have been caused by accumulation of capital, but Solow (1956) points out that, ultimately, diminishing returns to capital set in. This still leaves the possibility of convergence, a process by which poorer countries catch up with the average income of richer nations. Poor countries have a lower capital stock, and, for them, diminishing returns to capital may not have set in. The corollary is that they should grow more rapidly until they catch up with rich countries' per capita income. The true process, however, behind high growth, above the "natural" rate,[2] is technical progress (in machines and technology), which raises productivity – a process that is treated as exogenous in the neoclassical growth model. Technical progress is ultimately responsible for our historically high standards of living in rich countries. The new growth theories endogenize the process of technological change (see Romer 1990, for example), stating that technical progress is an externality, or, latterly, a phenomenon associated with increasing returns

---

1. This is akin to examining a production function in which output is a function of land, labour and capital, with a consideration for intermediate inputs such as energy and financial services.
2. The natural equilibrium growth rate is given by the growth rate of the effective labour force plus the depreciation rate of the capital stock requiring replacement.

to scale or monopolized research and development, allowing growth to be greater than the natural rate.

There is room for economic policies to promote growth: investment in skill and education, infrastructural development, openness to international trade, and so on. Moreover, the empirical evidence for convergence is weak; poor countries, on the whole, do not grow as rapidly as or more rapidly than rich countries, which is precisely why they are still poor. Thus, we have had "divergence, big time" (Pritchett 1997). In addition, growth-promoting policies have met with mixed success. Indeed, Easterly and Levine (2003) and Rodrik, Subramanian and Trebbi (2004) demonstrate that institutional quality differences are a better explanatory factor for differences in average income between countries compared to policies. Henceforth, the search for the long-term or deep determinants of growth commences!

There are three competing explanatory factors for the processes underlying long-run growth: culture, geography and institutions. Cultural explanations for growth can be traced back to Weber's (2010 [1905]) celebrated study, which argued that Protestantism instilled values essential to the development of capitalism. Other economic historians have also attempted to explain the Industrial Revolution in Britain as a consequence of the right value systems prevalent there. There is a powerful element of reverse causality between culture and growth, however, as both impact on each other. Culture may have an impact on economic growth, but, equally, economic growth alters cultural characteristics. Hence, one closely determines the other.

With regard to the more modern geographical explanations for economic development, Gallup, Sachs and Mellinger (1998) have argued that a tropical location, particularly a tropical African location, is disadvantageous to long-term growth. They contend that agricultural productivity is lower in sub-Saharan Africa, because of the lack of seasonal variation of the type present in more temperate climates. Second, Africa carried a greater disease burden, even before the AIDS pandemic, with the prevalence of especially virulent types of malaria. Finally, there is the feature of land-lockedness: a lot of the population of Africa live great distances from the sea, making it difficult to transport goods.

The problem with both the cultural and geographical explanations for growth is that they are immutable; nothing much can be done to change them in terms of policies. It literally takes centuries to alter culture, and millennia for geographical constraints to loosen. The historical reversal of fortune explanations of Acemoglu, Johnson and Robinson (2002) point out that, geographically speaking, the richer countries in AD 1500 were located near the tropics (China, for example), whereas nowadays they tend to be further away from the tropics in temperate zones, suggesting, at least, that geographical explanations for long-run growth can be turned on their head. This leaves us with the role of institutions in explaining long-term growth.

Acemoglu, Johnson and Robinson (2001, 2005) have produced the most influential recent theoretical basis for the role of institutions in determining long-term growth. They argue that political and economic institutions need to be differentiated. The latter are mainly related to property rights and contract enforcement, which are associated with the rule of law. Political institutions pertain both to formal rules (the constitution or long-established conventions) and to the informal exercise of power. Formal political institutions are slow to change, as evidenced by the infrequency with which constitutions are altered. Informal political institutions refer to the power of the influential, and are very much related to the distribution of income or wealth. Political institutions and the distribution of wealth are the two state variables that jointly determine economic institutions, which in turn determine economic performance or growth, and the future distribution of resources and political institutions. Furthermore, economic efficiency and the distribution of power or initial wealth are inseparable. This means that economically optimal policies, from the viewpoint of society at large, cannot always be implemented. Why, for example, is a group of dynamic businessmen unable to bribe those in power to pursue the right policies that promote investment? Because commitments made by rulers or sovereigns are not completely credible and can be reneged upon. These promises by rulers are essentially non-contractable, in the absence of credible constitutional anchors of commitment. So, for example, redistributive policies can anchor the democratic contract.

According to Acemoglu, Johnson and Robinson (2005), the conditions for the development of good economic institutions are threefold. First, when there are constraints on the executive and there is a balance of power present between different forces in society, implying a degree of democracy, along with a separation of powers. Nowadays most developing countries are imperfect democracies. Although many hold elections frequently, there are few checks on the elected executive. Consequently, they tend to exercise unbridled power when in office, and frequently adopt economic policies that enrich only narrow support groups. Second, when the enforcement of property rights (necessary to secure investment) is broad-based and not confined to an elite group's interests. Otherwise, predation will be common; violence is the easiest means of protecting the vast estates of the wealthy few. In other words, societies with less inequality and a powerful middle class are more likely to devise superior economic institutions. Finally, when there are few "rents" that can be appropriated by a small group – implying that the absence of rents that can be easily captured is also a condition for the emergence of more sound economic institutions. Resource rents can, therefore, hamper the development of good institutions, unless a strong history of institutional resilience checks these tendencies.

Acemoglu, Johnson and Robinson (2001, 2005) relate poor (or good) institutional determination to patterns of colonialization. They distinguish between two types of colonies. The first group corresponds to parts of the world settled by European migrants, as in North America and Australasia. The second group refers to tropical developing countries, today's Third World. The idea is that better institutions, especially property rights and the rule of law, were embedded in the first group.[3] In the second category of colonial countries, an extractive pattern of production was set up. This extractive and exploitative pattern of production is also the legacy of colonialization – malign colonialization, in these cases.

Clearly, this pattern was more prevalent in some parts of the world, particularly in Africa and Latin America. As the extractive state is expropriatory and predatory, bad institutions emerge and become entrenched even after independence, and a predatory equilibrium emerges. The important question that remains unanswered is this: why did decolonialization, and the opportunities it provides for policy changes, not alter the destiny of an extractive economy? It did for some, but not others. Second, despite the saliency of the colonial phase in history, many developing nations have had a collective experience prior to, and after, colonialization that must have also shaped institutions. In East Asia, South Asia, the Middle East and North African regions of the developing world, well-functioning institutions of good governance existed well before the advent of colonialization, and

---

3. The authors argue that the mortality rate amongst Europeans is what determined whether Europeans settled a colony or not.

European colonial powers merely adapted pre-existing administrative institutions. Indeed, it could be argued that post-independence leaders in these regions whose legitimacy was justified (at least partially) because of their efforts in Cold War battles against communism, or more recently the war on terror, have done considerable harm to institutions, especially democratic constraints on the executive and the separation of powers. Moreover, Glaeser *et al.* (2004) argue that what the settlers in North America and Australasia brought with them was not high-quality institutions but their high human capital.[4]

Another strand of the literature builds on the link between inequality and resource endowment of the point-sourced variety; see the work of Sokoloff and Engerman (2000), who discuss the historical experience of Latin America, and Easterly (2007) for a cross-sectional analysis across nations. Commodity endowments of the point source variety tend to depress the middle-class share of income in favour of elites, as in Latin America. The idea is that these elites, in turn, use their power, which is identical with the forces of the state, to coerce and extract rents. When different groups compete with another for these rents, the rent-seeking contest leads to even more perverse and wasteful outcomes than when elites collude. The important point made by Easterly (2007) is that small elite-based societies do not have a stake in the long-term development of the land. Unlike in middle-class-dominated societies, publicly financed human capital formation and infrastructural development falls by the wayside, thus depressing growth prospects.

Easterly's work is motivated by the theory in Bourguignon and Verdier (2000), whose model introduces the possibility of endogenous redistribution of income by an oligarchic elite leading to democracy. The reason is that mass education promotes growth, although it eventually dissipates the power of the existing elite. Education is costly, but it results in a private benefit for the educated (higher lifetime income), as well as an all-important growth-enhancing public benefit. The benefits from the latter effect also accrue to oligarchs. This may induce the selfish elite to redistribute income, as it allows the capital-constrained poor to obtain an education and contribute to rapid national economic development, even though this means the

---

4. They argue that the best predictor of high growth is the initial stock of human capital.

eventual loss of power for the oligarchy through the emergence of democracy. The important point is that a small oligarchy may be more disinclined to redistribute income, and this is more likely in point-sourced mineral- and plantation-based economies. By the same token, elites in resource-poor countries have a somewhat greater incentive to tolerate redistribution.

Resource rents and growth

A more technical review of this literature can be found in Deacon (2011). We may begin our summary of resource rents and harmful rent-seeking by referring to the theory of the optimal allocation of talent, as analysed in Murphy, Shleifer and Vishny (1991). The idea is that talent can focus either on production or on predation and corruption. This decision is a function of the relative returns to these two activities; predation may be more attractive when there is a wealth of natural resource rents. Capturable resource rents can lead to rent-seeking behaviour; revenues and royalties from oil or mineral resources are much more readily appropriable when compared to the income flows from agricultural commodities. Increases in the availability of resource rents following a boom in their world prices can increase the appetite for resource rents among certain individuals or groups within society. Baland and Francois (2000) model rent-seeking in the context of resource booms. The idea that rent-seeking and lobbying activities can detract from production can be traced back to Bhagwati (1982), where lobbying activities shrink the output available to the economy.

Lane and Tornell (1996) postulate that many societies have powerful interest groups that are coalitions formed in order to extract rents or a tribute from the rest of society. They could exist for historical reasons. Transfers to these groups are at the expense of others, and sometimes they even diminish the general productivity of the economy. Resource booms and windfalls increase the appetite for transfers within these powerful coalitions by a factor that is more than proportionate to the size of the boom. These groups become greedier, and demand an even larger share of national income. This is called the voracity effect by Lane and Tornell (1996); a similar mechanism is described as the rentier effect by Ross (2001). Furthermore, entrepreneurs may choose to become corrupt rent-seekers rather than engage in the ordinary business of production, and this constitutes a major diversion of talent away from production; see also Torvik (2002). Moreover, in some societies rent-seeking is more widespread than in others, depending on the institutional environment, referred to as grabber-friendly institutions by Mehlum, Moene and Torvik (2006), as opposed to producer-friendly institutions.

Hodler (2006) considers the effects of windfall resource rents in fractionalized societies. The windfall rents constitute a prize that is subject to a classic rent-seeking contest. Intense rent-seeking activities damage institutions of property rights in the non-resource sector. This reduces incentives for production in the non-resource sector, thereby harming aggregate output.

In Murshed's (2010: chap. 2) theoretical model, corruption or rent-seeking not only detracts from normal production but can even diminish the availability of productive capital over time, and a lower capital stock is what causes the eventual decline in growth. Unlike recent studies in this genre, it has explicit micro/macro theoretical properties, with an explicit macroeconomic model of growth collapse. A rent-seeking game is modelled, with the innovative feature that there can be increasing returns to scale in rent-seeking related to institutional quality. This means the returns to rent-seeking in certain institutional environments are huge. The worse the quality of institutions and the poorer the governance, the more profitable it is to engage in rent-seeking. Thus, not only is rent-seeking made explicitly endogenous to institutional quality but, innovatively, there can be increasing returns to scale in this activity. The extent of the rent-seeking also depends on the available quantity of capturable resource rents, as in Torvik (2002). This encourages more players to enter this game, with more wasteful consequences for the economy, including macroeconomic growth collapse (a sketch of this model is given in Appendix 1).

The political resource curse

Auty and Gelb (2001) construct a typology of states based on whether they are homogeneous or factional (several ethnic groups), as well as benevolent or predatory. A benevolent-developmental state, whether homogeneous (Indonesia, Northeast Asian countries) or factional (Botswana, Malaysia), tends to maximize social welfare and invest in infrastructure and human capital. Above all, a reliance on market forces, and competitive industrialization of a variety not relying on state subsidies, tends to emerge in the benevolent state. Within the benevolent category is the "paternalistic" variety, applicable to certain oil-rich countries (with a very high oil endowment per capita), such as Saudi Arabia, Brunei and Kuwait. These systems share some of the benevolent characteristics of developmental states that have been just mentioned, usually within the context of a consensual monarchy, but, unlike in the developmental state, less heed is paid to market forces. A predatory state promotes rent-seeking, lobbying and uncompetitive industrialization. The line of reasoning adopted in the Auty–Gelb (2001) typology does, indeed, go a long way in explaining the development successes of the last half a century, but we are left wondering: what *determines* the emergence of either of the two models and their associated institutions of governance?

All of this depends on the incentives that are presented to political leaders, because in certain circumstances they may choose unenlightened rent-seeking policies that suit them and a narrow interest group, and in a different environment they could decide to be more benevolent; see Auty and Gelb (2001). In both instances their behaviour is perfectly rational, except that in the former case it is in conflict with long-term national development. There is also the further possibility that they may deliberately undermine institutions and/or institutional development, so as to further their own ends.

Caselli and Cunningham (2007) outline a taxonomy of possible situations that shape rulers' incentives. It is based on (a) countries or institutional settings that are somewhat more centralized (ruled by a dictator or small elite) compared to decentralized cases (with wider political participation); and (b) when there is a budget constraint, in contrast to situations when there are no limits to resources to be spent; they also characterize situations (c) in which a public good needs to be provided (akin to Clarida & Findlay 1992), to increase the productivity of the non-resource productive sector; (d) when there is effort (creating moral hazard problems) that needs to be exercised by leaders; and (e) when leaders want to maximize rents accruing to themselves, and not national welfare, in the context of a limited probability of continuing in power. A sudden natural resource windfall increases the value of staying in power indefinitely, as there is more to loot at present and in the future. What happens then depends on leaders' incentives. Let us consider the different types of leaders and their motivations.

1. *The busy leader*: this is a constrained leader in a centralized system, who has to allocate effort in the sense of moral hazard into actions that lead to economic development and efforts to stay in power, which could include spending resources on political repression. An increase in natural resource revenues detracts from development effort, and cause a decline in per capita income. If the leader is unconstrained it raises the value of staying in power, and a resource boom will cause him to engage in more repression, although spending resources and effort on development also has a chance of increasing if both activities (repression and development) are complements. Similarly, political support and aid from the West during the Cold War and the present-day war on terror could tip the balance in favour of more repression relative to development effort. Note that political patronage in relatively decentralized and partially democratic systems can be a substitute both for repression and broad-based economic development. The question is, what cements relationships between patron and client: a common ethnicity based on religion, language or tribal affinity, or other forms of commitment devices, such as inefficient projects (as in Robinson & Torvik 2005)?

2. *The visionary leader*: this person may spend more resources on development if it increases his chances of survival, as was the case with President Suharto in Indonesia, but may do the opposite if it lowers the perceived probability of his survival, as was the case with Zaire's President Mobutu.

3. *A resigned leader*: this leader may see that following a resource boom his chances of future survival are low, because others will try to overthrow him, so that he becomes resigned. In effect, it has raised his discount rate for the future, and he will engage in less productive investment in development in order to survive.

4. *The lazy leader*: large windfalls, as in the Gulf, can give leaders enough resources to do everything. They may spend less time governing and more on leisure. Alternatively, in poorer countries they could let the rest of the country languish in poverty as long as they enjoy a lavish lifestyle.

Turning to how resource rents can affect institutions, Ross (2001) finds that countries rich in mineral resources, particularly oil, do not make a smooth transition to democracy – or, at least, their score on an index of democracy tends to be low. The reasons he identifies are the following. There is a lack of "modernization", as economic wealth does not translate into social and cultural change. Second, there is a repression effect: mineral and oil rich states can engage in higher levels of military and internal security expenditure to suppress dissent. Third, public goods are often provided alongside low taxes, because resource rents are the main source of revenue for the state; taxation normally results in eventual pressures from the taxed public to introduce democracy. Finally, and most importantly there is a *rentier* effect. Revenues from oil and mineral resources create rents that can be utilized to bribe the population into acquiescing to authoritarianism.

Caselli and Tesei (2016) argue that resource rents are more readily appropriable by a small group of elites in authoritarian developing countries. They argue that large increases in resource rents caused by commodity booms in resource-rich countries tend to strengthen the authoritarianism of established autocracies. This effect will be absent in relatively resource-poor economies, or in developing countries where democracy is already the norm. Large increases in resource rents provide ruling elites or oligarchies in established autocracies with extra resources to stave off political challenges by buying them off or investing in increased repression. The outcome depends greatly on the technology of repression, the degree of pliability of the citizenry and the extent of the subjective preferences of remaining in office. By contrast, resource booms will not advance autocratic tendencies in established democracies, such as Norway.

Collier and Hoeffler (2009) unpack democracy into (a) electoral competition and (b) checks and balances, and examine their interaction with natural resource rents (as a share of GDP) in determining GDP growth. The blend between resource rents and strong electoral competition is growth-reducing, while the mix of resource rents and strong checks and balances yield growth-enhancing outcomes. For example, they allude to the fact that, in resource-rich regions of Nigeria, strong electoral competition results in the elected executive avoiding taxation so as to circumvent the need for accountability to the electorate. They argue that, while the "neocon" agenda is to promote democracy through electoral competition, in fact what is needed are checks and balances on the executive.

Anderson and Askalen (2008) find that there is no resource curse for parliamentary democracies, in contrast to presidential systems. Although the result is an empirical finding, it also has theoretical overtones. Essentially, it is related to the fact that presidential systems concentrate more power in one person, and are therefore more factional and rent-seeking. The presidential system implies more rent extraction by politicians, a larger public sector and public spending targeted in favour of powerful groups rather than broad-based spending programmes. The problem with this work is that many so-called Westminster-style prime ministerial systems in the developing world are actually quite presidential in practice, as there is a weak separation of powers, combined with clientelism (patronage politics) and factionalism. Askalen and Torvik (2006) present a model of rent-seeking contests over natural resource rents that can lead a democracy into anarchy and civil war.

Robinson and Torvik (2005) also argue that increased resource rents encourage politicians in factional (such as those driven by tribal allegiances) or clientelist societies to invest in "white elephant" projects. These are projects that are inherently loss-making, but, once the sunk cost is incurred, the project is implemented. Despite the fact that they are loss-making and actually may be growth-retarding in the long term, they are nevertheless adopted because they act as a commitment device with the faction or support group essential to the politician's political survival via the mechanism of public employment.

Authors such as Karl (1999) have described the spending behaviour of oil rich economies as "petromania", referring to irresponsible consumption following oil booms. For example, it has been suggested that in Angola more than US$1 billion of oil revenues vanished per year through corruption in the period from 1996 to 2001. More generally, a wealth of mineral resources or plantation-based production can spawn extractive and non-developmental institutions that eventually become entrenched (Sokoloff & Engerman 2000).

Acemoglu and Robinson (2006) model underdevelopment as caused by political elites blocking technological and institutional development because such developments may erode the elites' incumbency advantage. This is more likely when rents from maintaining power are high, such as when public income is derived from natural resources. Robinson, Verdier and Torvik (2006) show how politicians have a short time horizon because they discount the future by the probability that they remain in power, which is damaging from a social perspective. With more resources, the future utility of having political power will increase, and, as a result, politicians will change policies so that the probability they remain in power increases. To do so they create a bloated public sector, rather like the "white elephants" in Robinson and Torvik (2005).

Bulte and Damania (2008) model the government's supply of a public good input to a resource sector and a competing "productive" sector based on political contributions made to government that enables it to stay in office. Here a resource boom can lead to an increase in the political contributions made by this sector relative to the more productive sector, engendering an economic resource curse akin to Dutch disease.

Finally, mention needs to be made about the "selectorate" notion of Bueno de Mesquita et al. (2003). This refers to the trade-off faced by those in power between supplying non-rivalled and non-excludable public goods to the citizenry at large in contrast to providing only their own support group with rents or targeted transfers. The support group or winning coalition is referred to as the selectorate. Furthermore, the smaller the winning coalition or selectorate, the greater the probability of the state making targeted transfers relative to supplying public goods to the ordinary citizen. Smith (2008) points out that in such a framework a resource windfall raises the average citizen's expectation of receiving a share of the windfall via public goods. In principle, this should expand the selectorate, but in pre-existing small coalitions it raises the probability of revolt, with a civil war risk implication.

Other negative effects of resource rents: education, savings and fiscal dependence

The importance of human capital in fostering economic growth and human development cannot be overemphasized. This relates to educational spending, mainly public expenditure on education. Resource rents and oil windfalls should, in principle, provide governments of developing countries with extra resources to invest in education. In contrast, there is the idea that in foreign-exchange-abundant resource-rich countries there is little incentive to invest in basic skills, as there is little need to have a skilled workforce to export processed goods. A good chunk of the educational expenditure will therefore be devoted to elite tertiary education. Again, there are many ways of measuring educational variables (Stijns 2006), such as the average years of schooling, the net secondary enrolment rate and public spending as a proportion of aggregate spending, or government spending on education as a proportion of total government expenditure.

Birdsall, Pinckney and Sabot (2001) show that resource abundance measured by cropland per capita systematically lowers public investment in education. Similarly, Gylfason (2001) shows that natural-resource-rich countries spend less on education in terms of expected years of schooling for girls, gross secondary enrolment rates and public expenditure on education as a proportion of national income. But these results are flawed, because his measure of natural resource abundance is defined incorrectly as the share of natural capital as a proportion of all types of capital; this biases downwards the resource abundance of high-income and successful countries in this category, simply because they have high stocks of all types of capital in the denominator relative to natural capital in the numerator.

In contrast to Birdsall, Pinckney and Sabot (2001) and Gylfason (2001), Stijns (2006) finds that, for developing countries, many of the measures of natural resource abundance can cause greater educational attainment and spending, as well as a higher life expectancy at birth. So, natural resource endowments may not be so bad for human development. There are several exceptions, however, depending on how we measure natural resource dependence or intensity. Countries with a high share of mineral exports in total exports fare badly, as do countries with a high ratio of natural to physical capital. Similarly, nations with a high ratio of green capital (non-arable forests, pasturelands, etc.) to physical capital, high agricultural export intensity and arable land per capita are also poor performers in this regard. These nations may be described as unsuccessful resource-abundant developing countries, and they include some agricultural exporters, as well as pastoralist countries in sub-Saharan Africa. A high primary or mineral export dependence means that a country has not diversified or industrialized; otherwise, it would have been exporting more processed manufactures, as is the case with resource-rich Malaysia. In addition, having a high natural or green capital endowment relative to produced capital is another sign of economic stagnation and the failure to develop, as development leads to a higher stock of physical capital via investment. Moreover, it appears that high proportions of cropland and timber wealth relative to physical capital stocks are worse for education and health indicators than high ratios of oil wealth to physical capital stocks. Furthermore, there are also no signs of countries systematically favouring tertiary over secondary education. The more recent study by Cockx and Francken (2016) indicates once more a negative public education spending effect of resource rents.

Metcalfe (2007) finds that the transmission mechanisms causing the resource curse are external indebtedness and poor institutional quality, measured by constraints on the executive. It may be that certain resource-rich countries with poorer institutional environments borrowed unsustainably during or shortly after booms in commodity prices. Moradbeigi and Law (2016) find that, in a sample of 63 countries for the period from 2000 to 2010, volatility in oil prices had a negative impact on growth fluctuations – an effect that could be moderated by financial development.

They may have also had lower resource-adjusted savings rates, as emphasized in Matsen and Torvik (2005). The debt overhang ensued after commodity prices collapsed in the 1980s, when these countries found it hard to service their debt; this jeopardized domestic investment and growth. These very same nations had perhaps made unwise domestic investments in less productive areas that did not aid future growth prospects. Once again, there are successful and unsuccessful resource-abundant nations. The fact that adjusted genuine savings (national savings plus education expenditure minus natural resource depletion) is negatively correlated with resource rents (market value minus extraction cost) in resource-rich countries is highlighted in Venables (2016). This is chiefly a result of the depletion of natural capital. This may be due to the fact that natural resources are not viewed as (natural) capital assets but as a source of income. Moreover, Bornhorst, Thornton and Gupta (2008) find a statistically significant negative relationship between the presence of hydrocarbon (oil and gas) revenues and other sources of government revenue in a panel of 30 hydrocarbon-producing nations. Thus, oil and gas in particular, but also resource rents, could hinder fiscal development. On a related matter, Bhattacharya and Hodler (2014) find that financial development is not hindered by resource revenues provided the institutional structure is sound.

This chapter has reviewed the theoretical literature linking resource rents to the lack of economic growth, as well as its role in promoting corruption, autocracy and poor institutions more generally. The theoretical literature in this context is dominated by models of rent-seeking behaviour. As stated earlier, the politics and the economics of the resource curse are inseparable, because poor economic policy choices hamper growth, but these decisions are always made in the context of a set of political institutions and the overall quality of governance. The manner in which resource rents are managed will also shape the quality of institutions, and from there on determine future economic performance. The next question that arises is how these theoretical propositions work in practice. In order to answer this question, we need to examine the empirical evidence on the resource curse, which is the subject of the next chapter.

4

Empirical evidence on the resource curse

This chapter examines the empirical evidence on the effects of resource rents, and whether they turn into a "curse" for the economy. There is an abundance of empirical research examining evidence for the existence of the resource curse, as indicated in Chapter 1. As far as the economics discipline is concerned, some of these studies involve cross-country econometric analysis, others look at the problem in a subnational context, and then there are more descriptive country case studies. I begin with measurement issues concerning important variables in this connection. This is followed by a survey of the cross-country econometric evidence regarding growth and resource rents, including literature that regards institutions as playing an important mediating role in growth, along the lines of Acemoglu, Johnson and Robinson (2001, 2005). The next section is concerned with the impact of resource rents on institutions, mainly in terms of democracy, but also corruption at a cross-country level. The cross-country econometric results are extremely variable as to whether there is a curse or not, depending on a whole host of factors, such as choice of variables (covariates), measures of resource richness chosen and also uses of evolving econometric techniques. Results using dynamic panel data analysis are considered the most reliable under the present state of the art in econometrics. I then review the subnational evidence on the resource curse when resource rents negatively impact on resource-producing regions relative to the rest of the national economy. Finally, I briefly examine a few country case studies of resource-rich economies, with some nations avoiding the resource curse, whereas others do not.

Measurement issues

It is worthwhile defining how resource intensity is measured. This can be important, as the ranking among nations with regard to resource dependence might change, depending upon the metric utilized. Furthermore, different units of measurement may cause fluctuating statistical significance in empirical models analysing the effect of resource abundance on other economic phenomena, such as growth or education spending. One way of measuring resource dependence would be simply to look at the proportionate contribution of mining (or mining and agriculture) in national income. This is the share of national income method. But a large mining sector does not necessarily imply economic dependence, as the economy might still be quite diversified with a large manufacturing share in national income.

This brings us to the second method, which would be based on the pattern of exports. We could look at the principal exports of the economy. Alternatively, one could use the share of primary (all unprocessed) or mineral exports in GDP as a measure. This would be an export intensity measure. The Sachs and Warner (1995, 1999a, 1999b, 2001) measures of the share of primary exports in GDP have been heavily criticized in recent years, as a measure of resource dependence and not abundance, and reflective of an already weak and undiversified economy. In addition, one might want to look at the share of minerals or energy in total exports. Murshed and Serino (2011) employ a variety of export concentration measures that gauge comparative advantage, the degree of diversification of a country's trade, its ability to export goods that are highly in demand in world trade, the extent of intra-industry trade and the degree to which natural-resource-based products are crude materials or *processed* through manufacturing.

A third type of measurement of resource abundance could look at stocks, say per capita stocks (for example, of oil reserves or other minerals), and not flows (of oil exports, say), giving us a measure of national per capita endowment of the value of these stocks. This may be a superior measure of resource abundance, but, as van der Ploeg and Poelhekke (2010) point out, the *stock* of natural resource assets is also related to the *flow* of rents emanating from these.

A fourth method is to look at ratios of total stocks of different types of capital. We could look at the ratio of natural to physical capital stocks. But, as Stijns (2006) points out, it would be problematic, if not gravely erroneous, to look at natural capital stocks as a proportion of *all types of capital stocks* (the sum of human, physical and natural capital), as in Gylfason (2001). So, a country such as Norway, which successfully invested in the past in education and infrastructure, would be classified as resource-poor simply because it has a high stock of total capital in the denominator of the ratio! Equally, an oil-rich developing country (because of low stocks of human and physical capital) would be classified as resource-rich simply because of the smallness of the denominator of the ratio relative to the numerator.

A fifth metric is associated with resource rents. "Rent" refers to the difference between prices and costs, giving us a measure of "excess" profit. This in turn can be calculated in per capita terms, or measured as a share of national income. Rents increase when there are booms in commodity prices, declining thereafter, and resource-rich countries suffer from this volatility. Finally, if we wanted to look at agricultural potential we could look at arable land per capita; see Auty (1997).

In order to gauge an economy's *dependence* on natural resources, some sort of export-based measure is most appropriate, as it conveys information about where a country's comparative or competitive advantage lies; see Brunnschweiler and Bulte (2008). Alternatively, as a measure of *intensity*, perhaps the ratio of natural capital to physical or human capital stocks (but not both) could be used, as it gives us an idea of how resource rents have been used to accumulate other types of capital; a low ratio would indicate earlier investment in other forms of capital.

Turning now to institutional data, we need to distinguish between measurements that are outcome-based, focusing mainly on governance, and those that refer to institutional process, usually the political system of a nation.

With regard to the first, the Kaufmann, Kraay and Mastruzzi (2006) is one example of governance indicators. These correspond most closely to the aforementioned economic institutions. The rankings are for voice and accountability, political stability, government effectiveness, regulatory quality, rule of law and control of corruption. They extend from –2.5, at the lower end of the spectrum, to 2.5, at the upper end. The implication also is that a positive score is good and a negative score is below average. The scores are highly correlated with per capita income.[1] Most developing countries, particularly low-income nations, score negatively in these areas.

Other examples of sources of data on governance include the Fraser Institute[2] and the International Country Risk Guide (ICRG).[3] The economic freedom index of the Fraser Institute consists of five major components: (a) size of government and taxation; (b) private property and the rule of law; (c) sound money; (d) trade regulation and tariffs; and (e) regulation of business, labour and capital markets. This index has a maximum score of 10. The composite or aggregate ICRG index consists of three broad categories of indicators: political, financial and economic risk. The latter two categories of variables are akin to macroeconomic indicators of debt, exchange rate instability, and so on. The ICRG political risk categories have subcomponents of institutional quality: government stability, corruption, law and order, investment profile and bureaucracy quality.

As far as political-process-based institutions are concerned, the most commonly used data set refers to democracy, and is known as the Polity index.[4] This data set gives a democracy score on an upward scale of 0 to 10 (with Western democracies scoring 10). A truly meaningful democracy is arrived at only with a Polity score of 8. The autocracy data set gives an autocracy score of between −10 (highest) and 0 (lowest). The Polity 2 or 4 score is a combination of both autocracy and democracy, and a reflection of a country's democratic or non-democratic status. Most developing countries occupy an indeterminate zone, and are neither democracies nor autocracies, but have characteristics of both (electoral competition along with weak constraints on the executive), occupying a position on the Polity scale of between, say, −4 and 4. These countries are known as "anocracies". The Polity database also has information on constraints on the executive and the openness, as well as competiveness, of executive recruitment.

---

1. This illustrates the reverse causality or endogeneity problem that exists between institutions and growth. Good institutions may promote growth, but growth also leads to institutional improvement.
2. See www.fraser institute.org/economic-freedom/dataset (accessed 30 July 2018).
3. See https://epub.prsgroup.com/products/international-country-risk-guide-icrg (accessed 30 July 2018).
4. See www.cidcm.umd.edu/insr/polity (accessed 30 July 2018).

Mention should be made of the new V-Dem or varieties of democracy data set.[5] Being new, and very detailed, the period covered by the data set is more limited than Polity. Compared to Polity, the V-Dem data set is more finely grained, rich in varieties of components, and does not focus only on electoral processes, as Polity tends to do. There are teams of country experts comprising nationals from the countries concerned. The data set has also the advantage that it can be used to look at the dynamics of movements across recent times. The data has many components and subcomponents. There is the liberal component index, covering freedom of expression, judicial constraints on the executive and legislative constraints on the executive subindices. The electoral democracy index has freedom of expression, association and clean election, among other subcomponents. Interestingly, there is an egalitarian component index, with indices of equal protection, equal access and equal distribution of resources. It also has a participatory component index, with indices of local and regional government, and a deliberative component index, with measures ranging from respect for counter-arguments to the range of consultation. All in all, this should prove to be a much superior measure of political processes, but its newness and novelty mean that its application is still limited.

Cross-country evidence: resource rents and growth

The focus in this subsection is on growth, but nearly every empirical cross-country econometric study on the effect of resource rents on growth allows for a mediating role for institutions, either by interacting resource rents with institutional quality or by first estimating the effect of natural resources on institutions, then looking at the effect of the estimated institutions on growth. The definition of institutions, the natural resource abundance or dependence variable definitions, the period of analysis and the econometric technique (pure cross-section, panel data, panel data with fixed or random effects, dynamic panel or time series techniques) all matter to the results.

Mehlum, Moene and Torvik (2006) find that, when they interact natural resource abundance with the quality of institutions in a growth regression,

---

5.   See www.v-dem.net (accessed 30 July 2018).

the resultant coefficient is significant. This means that natural resource abundance has adverse effects *only* in the presence of poor institutions. Their analysis is purely cross-sectional, however, and they do not take into account the potential reverse causality between institutional quality and growth (both of which have a causal effect on the other).

In a purely cross-sectional econometric analysis, Isham *et al.* (2005) find that point-sourced economies identified as exporters of oil, minerals and plantation-based crops have lower growth rates compared to diffuse (agricultural) and manufactured exporters in the 1975–97 period because of the poorer governance (based on the Kaufmann indicators of good governance mentioned above) engendered by a fuel-, mineral- or plantation-dependent economy. The challenge is to extend the pure cross-sectional econometric analysis so that it has a time dimension, and delve deeper into the role of different types of resource endowment on institutional formation.

The Mavrotas, Murshed and Torres (2011) estimation was one of the earlier panel data econometric analyses in this connection, including the use of dynamic panel data methods, involving generalized method of moments (GMM) estimations. As with Isham *et al.* (2005), they instrument for endogeneity problems. Their results suggest that both point source and diffuse-type natural resource endowments retard the development of democracy (measured by Polity) and good governance (from the economic freedom index, EFI database), which in turn hampers economic growth. Thus there is a more widespread resource curse, valid for both endowment types. Point-sourced economies have a worse impact on governance, and governance is more important for growth compared to democracy. Diffuse economies appear to slow down democratic development fractionally more than point-sourced economies; we should not be tempted into concluding that point-sourced endowments are better for democratic development, however, because that is patently not the case. The resource curse of point-sourced dependence definitely looms large, as it is more growth-retarding via even poorer governance than diffuse natural resources. Manufacturing, and manufactured goods exports, do promote better governance and democracy. This in turn helps to explain the superior growth performance of manufactured-goods-exporting nations. Not only is the presence of manufactured exports an indication of a more diversified and growing economy, but this may be so because these countries have better institutions of governance and higher levels of democracy.

Murshed and Serino (2011) employ disaggregated trade data sets to elaborate sophisticated measures of trade specialization that distinguish between unprocessed and manufactured natural resource products and are informative about countries' trade diversification experience, their link to world demand trends and involvement in intra-industry trade. Using panel data (GMM) methods they find that it is mainly specialization in natural resource products with little or no processing that slows down economic growth, as it impedes the emergence of more dynamic patterns of trade specialization. These findings imply that the key to escaping the so-called resource curse is economic diversification, which can be initiated by increasing the degree of natural resource processing. Their results hold true after controlling for institutional quality (Polity and the rule of law).

Brunnschweiler and Bulte (2008), in a cross-sectional analysis, differentiate between resource dependence and resource abundance.[6] Their measures of resource dependence are resource exports to GDP and mineral exports to GDP; the per capita value of natural resource and subsoil asset stocks is their resource abundance variable. They instrument for endogeneity issues in both resource dependence and institutions: the constitution (presidential versus parliamentarian) and trade openness for resource dependence, and absolute latitude for institutions. They find that resource *dependence* has no significant effect on growth (although the sign is still negative), contrary to many earlier findings regarding the resource curse. By contrast, they find that resource *abundance* has significantly positive effects on growth, either *directly* in a growth regression or *indirectly* through institutional improvements (measured by the rule of law and government effectiveness from the Kaufmann data set). In short, greater resource abundance leads to better-quality institutions and more rapid growth, a counter-intuitive finding that is echoed by Smith (2004) in his findings about oil wealth and its negative relation to repression and positive relation to regime survival. Their results were criticized by van der Ploeg and Poelhekke (2010), however, on the grounds that the resource abundance variable is not truly exogenous, but endogenous to resource dependence (exports of primary goods), and for other potentially important missing independent variables.

---

6. Norman (2009) also distinguishes between resource abundance and resource intensity, similar to the notion of resource dependence.

In many ways the Brunnschweiler and Bulte (2008) results are understandable when one makes a distinction between resource abundance and dependence. As pointed out earlier, a resource-abundant nation may not be very resource-dependent, if it has wisely chosen to, and has had time to, diversify its production structure through economic growth, which also raises the living standards of the citizenry. Indeed, resource dependence may be a reflection of the failure to grow and develop good economic and political institutions, along with the associated poverty, inequality and poor human development outcomes.

Collier and Goderis (2007) use an error correction panel data regression model, which is dynamic and also addresses reverse causality, to differentiate long-run and short-run effects of commodity price booms on economic growth. They find that commodity booms have a positive short-term effect on output, but adverse long-term effects. The long-term effects are confined to "high-rent", non-agricultural commodities, by differentiating commodity prices between agricultural (diffuse) and non-agricultural (point) goods. Within the latter group, they also find that the resource curse is avoided by countries with sufficiently good institutions, by (a) including an interaction term between the commodity price index and a dummy for good institutions (with Portugal as the benchmark) and (b) separating the regressions into two groups that differentiate countries with bad and good governance.

Boschini, Petterson and Roine (2013) in their taxonomic study distinguish between different types of institutions and also use recent innovations in panel data econometrics to gauge whether good institutions can reverse the natural resource curse on growth. They allow for the endogeneity of institutions in some instances, but not those related to natural resource abundance or dependence, and try out different measures of resource dependence including rents, exports, export share in GDP, as well as differentiating between different types of natural resources. Similar to the study by Metcalfe (2007), the resource curse seems to get weaker in recent years, and the results for the effect of different institutions (chiefly Polity and ICRG) are not always robust to different specifications, periods and samples, except for the ICRG governance-type institutions for metals and ores (but not fuel) exporters. Kim and Lin (2017), using heterogeneous panel cointegration techniques, do find evidence for a growth resource curse, but one that is mediated by the quality of institutions. Sarmidi, Law and Jafari (2014) find an institutional quality threshold effect in the natural resource and economic growth relationship.

In other words, natural resources meaningfully impact on growth only after a certain threshold of institutional quality has been arrived at.

Murshed, Badiuzzaman and Pulok (2015) investigate the relationship between natural resource dependence and economic growth via institutional development, employing two sets of cross-country panels. The first panel comprises up to 63 developing countries for the period from 1970 to 2010, and the second panel consists of 86 developing countries over the more recent period from 1995 to 2012. The methodology is similar to Mavrotas, Murshed and Torres (2011). Their results indicate that governance matters more in determining economic progress compared to democratic development in the longer term, in line with the findings of Mavrotas, Murshed and Torres (2011). This means that economic institutions are more salient compared to purely process-oriented political institutions. A similar result is produced by Kolstad (2009), who finds that the rule of law matters more than democracy. Within the category of political institutions, constraints on the executive may be more important than the degree of democracy, as the former may be more central in generating more accountable and less corrupt government. Murshed, Badiuzzaman and Pulok (2015) also find that the more outcome-based governance indicators, such as corruption and investment profile, are less significant than more process-led institutions of governance, such as government stability, the quality of the bureaucracy and law and order, as well as the conduct of tax, trade, fiscal and monetary policies contained within the EFI. They validate another finding of Mavrotas, Murshed and Torres (2011): the more harmful impact of point commodity exports compared to diffuse product exports on institutional development is much less than was previously thought.

Interestingly, there is evidence of a reversal of the institutional decline engendered by resource dependence in the recent post-Cold-War era in line with the findings of Metcalfe (2007) and Boschini, Petterson and Roine (2013). Apergis and Payne (2014) find that, for the countries of the Middle East and North Africa (MENA), oil revenues had negative effects on growth in the period from 1990 to 2003, but that this effect moderated afterwards. Mehrara (2009) finds a threshold effect for oil rent effects on growth in a sample of 13 countries between 1965 and 2005. After an initial annual growth rate of 18 to 19 per cent, oil revenues began to exert a negative effect on growth.

As far as methodological innovation is concerned, Smith (2015) uses a treatment-type effect of natural resource discoveries from 1950 in countries which experienced this phenomenon (resource discovery, hence treated) compared to a control group of resource-poor countries, excluding those nations that were already resource-rich in 1950. The author utilizes panel fixed effects, as well as synthetic control analysis as a further robustness check for his results. The results indicate that natural resource discoveries in developing countries have a positive effect on per capita income growth, education and infant mortality reduction. The impact on democratic institutions is negative, however, and – crucially – the economies remain undiversified, pointing to potentially serious problems when the economies run out of natural resources.

When applying the meta-analysis technique to the natural resource to growth nexus literature, Havránek, Horváth and Zeynalov (2016)[7] discover a non-consensual literature after they correct for publication biases. Some 40 per cent find a negative effect of resource rents, and about 20 per cent obtain positive effects, with the remaining 40 per cent getting no significant effect. When they look at the effect of different types of resources they find that oil can have a more positive impact on growth compared to other resources. The paper concludes that the emphasis must lie in the importance of institutions as a mediating factor in this process, and with improved institutions the resource curse is largely absent.

Cross-country evidence: resource rents and institutions

I intend to focus mainly on studies that examine the direct impact of natural resources on institutions; mainly on corruption, a governance outcome variable and process-oriented democracy. While there are many data sets on corruption, most authors use the Polity combined democracy/autocracy score described above as their metric for democracy, or, alternatively, other Polity data such as constraints on the executive. To my knowledge, no analysis using the V-Dem data on the resource curse exists. Once again, the econometric technique, the definition of natural resources and the period of analysis matter.

---

7.   The authors examine 402 econometric estimates in 33 separate studies.

A study by Busse and Gröning (2013), using contemporary dynamic panel data analysis, finds that the natural resource export share of GDP negatively impacts on institutions drawn from the ICRG, especially corruption. For other governance variables, such as bureaucratic quality, they do find negative effects, but not robustly to all specifications. As far as law and order is concerned, the results are mostly statistically insignificant. Williams (2011), using dynamic panel data econometric techniques (system GMM), finds that point-resource-type exports exert a negative impact on transparency and the release of information. When controlling for the impact of transparency or other institutions (informational transparency, executive constraints and the International Country Risk Guide), the sign and significance of the negative effect of point natural resources on growth diminishes, suggesting that the impact of resource dependence on growth is via institutional functioning.

On the issue of female participation in the labour force, Ross (2008) finds that oil rents and an oil-dependent economy result in lower female participation in the labour force and, consequently, less female representation in politics (measured by the number of women legislators, say).[8] In economies with a somewhat larger contribution from manufacturing there is greater gender parity, measured by higher female participation in the labour force and female representation in politics.

Arezki and Brückner (2011) study the effect of oil rents (applying individual country discount factors) on corruption (ICRG) for a panel of 31 countries from 1992 to 2005 using panel data and dynamic panel data methods. Increases in oil rents do significantly increase corruption when the state (and therefore elite groups) has greater ownership of oil production and rents. But at the same time civil liberties increase, while political rights, as defined by Freedom House (EFI), decline, which the authors argue is related to state ownership of oil. When there is state ownership of oil, the rents are controlled by elites who raise civil liberties to avoid conflict but restrict political rights to avoid redistributive pressures. The effects on Polity democracy scores are not significant. Bhattacharyya and Hodler (2010) use panel data for 124 countries in the period 1980 to 2004 to test

---

8. Ross (2008) further demonstrates that this effect is not due to the prevalence of Islam in major Middle Eastern oil-exporting nations but, rather, the dominance of oil in the economy.

if resource rents (not just oil) increase corruption (again from the ICRG), and find that they do so only if democratic institutions (Polity democracy/ autocracy scores) are weak. Oil rents, in particular, have been closely related to corruption; see, for example, the country case studies in the political ecology tradition in the edited volume by Williams and Le Billon (2017).

Vicente (2010) uses the natural experimental technique[9] to evaluate the rise in corruption in São Tomé and Príncipe following oil discoveries there. As a control group he used Cape Verde, a nation sharing many common characteristics, including the fact that they were both Portuguese colonies for the same length of time. Using retroactive surveys of citizen's subjective perceptions about corruption before and after the advent of oil revenues in São Tomé and Príncipe. Simultaneous surveys on corruption were conducted in Cape Verde. In addition to the natural experiment of the oil revenue treatment, the surveys on corruption perceptions, before and after oil revenues came on stream, permitted a difference-in-difference impact analysis of the introduction of oil revenues. A significant rise in corruption in several categories was estimated. Vicente (2010) has also developed indicators of whether citizens were highly informed or not, enabling triple difference estimates, reinforcing the earlier difference-in-difference results.[10]

The previous chapter described how oil in particular, but natural resource rents in general, may retard democratic development via a rentier effect, and the lack of a demand for accountability for the executive in the absence of non-oil taxes, the absence of modernization and a repression effect. In other words, substantial resource rents in general, and oil rents in particular, encourage authoritarianism, even if it is of a benevolent variety. We have noted that Ross (2001) finds that in oil-rich economies the process of democratic development is slow or absent, especially in the oil-rich Arab countries. Smith (2004) finds that oil-rich economies exhibit a great deal of political regime durability, arguing that the stability of the political system cannot be accounted for by repression, but that oil economies form stable

9. In experimental economics (as in medical randomized control trials) there has to be a control group who are not treated, in addition to the treatment group. Both groups should have highly similar characteristics, apart from the fact that the treatment group is "treated" but the control group is not treated. Subjects in both groups need to be chosen randomly.
10. Difference-in-difference methodologies attempt to gauge the *difference* the treatment has made to the outcome.

domestic coalitions, implying the absence of strongly negative rentier-type effects. The subject is, therefore, empirically controversial, with no consensus emerging either way in the literature.

Tsui (2011) focuses on oil *discoveries*, finding that large oil discoveries in absolute (not necessarily in per capita) terms, and where the quality of the crude oil is high and extraction costs are low, does retard democratic development, as measured by Polity. Aslaksen (2010) shows that the relationship between oil rents and democracy is negative even when country fixed effects are taken into consideration, ironing out unobserved heterogeneity at the country level. Among the dissenting findings is Wacziarag (2012), who does not find this to be the case. An influential study by Haber and Menaldo (2011) using time series econometrics finds that the findings by Ross (2001) about oil hindering democracy are not statistically significant. In retort, Andersen and Ross (2014) argue that this result is not applicable to developing countries in the post-1980 period, when oil resources became more state-owned and prone to elite capture. Prior to 1980 the prevalence of Western multinational oil companies was greater. The study by Blanco, O'Connor and Nugent (2016), who also used advanced time series techniques, is more supportive of Haber and Menaldo (2011), suggesting that oil does *not* hinder democracy. A meta-analysis by Ahmadov (2014) finds that there may be a small but significant negative effect of oil on democracy. This negative effect on democracy may be stronger in the Middle East and North Africa, but it is positive for Latin America.

As noted in the previous chapter, Caselli and Tesei (2016) find that resource rent *windfalls*, which typically occur during commodity price booms, encourage authoritarianism, measured by the Polity scale; in countries that are autocracies, there is pressure to move towards greater autocracy, the more so the less the degree of autocracy was initially. Resource rent windfalls have little impact on countries that are already democracies in this connection. The findings are robust to a variety of techniques, including GMM techniques, as well as commodity classifications.

Within-country evidence

As indicated above, the growing within-country or subnational resource curse literature examines whether the resource-rich or resource-producing region is disadvantaged in comparison to its resource-poor counterparts by resource rents; see Cust and Viale (2016) for a review. By "subnational" we mean that the unit of analysis is a state or province within a country, with some studies going down to the finer district or county level. This literature compares resource-poor and resource-rich regions.[11] Among the problems encountered is the environmental footprint of resource production, a discussion on which is beyond the scope of this work. Other problems are associated with the inability of regional governments to manage the revenues generated, in a growing environment of fiscal federalism and decentralized revenue management. The citizens of a resource-producing region are frequently disgruntled with their lack of control over locally generated revenues. This can be a major cause of conflict, secessionism and civil war, as we shall see in the next chapter.

One effect could be that the resource-rich region grows less rapidly than its poorer counterparts. For the United States, a study by Allcott and Keniston (2014), utilizing panel data at the county level to compare the economic performance for oil and gas regions, finds that they have poorer growth rates. This finding is contradicted by a study by Michaels (2011), who finds that, because of the agglomeration benefits of oil and gas production, resource-producing counties are better off. At the state level, however, Papyrakis and Gerlagh (2007) demonstrate that resource-rich US states lag behind poorer ones on account of lower investment, lower educational attainment and lower trade openness. For Canada, Papyrakis and Raveh (2014) find classic Dutch disease effects: mineral-rich regions suffered from greater inflationary pressures and reduced competitiveness, with a relatively large non-traded sector.

In China, Zhang *et al.* (2007) show that resource-rich regions do more poorly than resource-poor regions in terms of consumption growth, with the transmission mechanism being rises in the local price of non-traded goods, which damage the competitiveness of local firms. They also point to the problem of property rights, which means that resource rents are mainly grabbed by state-owned enterprises or the state. In India, Asher and Novosad (2013) demonstrate that areas with mining have smaller manufacturing sectors. This is also found for Indonesia by Cust (2015), who

---

11. I do not review the literature on *individual*, localized case studies in this subsection.

finds that, in a 15 kilometre radius, there is an increase in service sector employment. Dutch disease effects lower regional competitiveness in traded goods (manufacturing, agriculture) but can be mitigated by a more enabling business environment, infrastructural development and migration policies to ease local labour shortages.

An interesting study of gold-mining regions in Peru by Aragón and Rud (2013) also points to regional Dutch disease effects, increasing local wage rates of employees working in infrastructural projects – something that has come to be known as the Peruvian disease. There is (circumstantial) evidence of corruption at the local level as well; Caselli and Michaels (2013) find that oil windfalls in Brazil had no impact on education and health supply locally, pointing to the purloining of funds. Resource rent windfalls can also negatively impact on the way citizens hold politicians accountable, as found in an experimental study in an Indonesian resource rich region (Paler 2013).

In summary, evidence of resource rents impacting negatively on local competitiveness or a subnational Dutch disease is mixed. There are two further issues requiring consideration, however. The first is to do with local grievances produced by resource rents when citizens think they do not get a fair share of these; this can produce conflict, and is examined in the next chapter. Second, local governance needs improvement so as to manage revenues in a superior fashion, avoiding corruption and rent-seeking. Revenue-sharing mechanisms between the national and local governments need to be fine-tuned in this context. As argued by Cust and Viale (2016), there are other considerations, including permitting local governments to bank their current resource revenue surpluses for use in future financial years. A further policy implication is the lowering of corruption to prevent the misappropriation of funds.

Country case studies

Although cross-sectional econometric evidence is reliable, we have seen how mixed these results are, and sensitive to econometric technique, data coverage, dependent variable definition and the choice of independent variables for inclusion in the analysis. Additionally, the results indicate an average outcome across all nations, and do not always highlight the country specificities causing success or failure in the wake of resource discoveries or booms. Consequently, a brief outline of some country cases in either avoiding or succumbing to the resource curse may be a useful exercise. In what follows I describe six country cases, two each from Asia, Africa and Latin America. This makes my choice of countries somewhat geographically representative. Furthermore, each continent is represented by one success at avoiding the resource curse, and one relative failure in doing so. The countries in question are Malaysia, Saudi Arabia, Botswana, Nigeria, Chile and Bolivia. I have also avoided discussing nations afflicted by major secessionist civil wars since the end of the Cold War.[12]

Before delving into the country cases, it is worthwhile looking at some pair-wise or multi-country country comparisons. Dunning (2005) analyses choices by rulers regarding the future growth path of the economy in the context of natural resource abundance. He compares Mobutu's Zaire (1965–97) to Suharto's Indonesia (1965–98) and Botswana during the same period. In Botswana revenues from Kimberlite (deep mineshaft) diamonds were very stable, as a result of Botswana's unique relationship with the South African diamond company De Beers and its important position as a major supplier. It did not need to diversify its economy. But it chose a developmental path because of the mature nature of political elites there. In Indonesia and Zaire resource flows were volatile. In one case the dictator (Suharto) chose diversification and growth-enhancing strategies, as well as policies aimed at equalization and poverty reduction to contain political opposition. In the other case (Zaire, now the Democratic Republic of Congo: DRC), Mobutu did not, because he felt that diversification and investment in infrastructure would loosen his grip on power and strengthen political opposition to him based on ethnicity. The same has been argued for Nkrumah in Ghana. Both Mobutu and Suharto, in particular, owed their existence, at least initially, to the patronage of the United States and Western powers. Perhaps in East Asia greater fears of communism strengthened benevolence in dictators (South Korea, Taiwan, Singapore and Indonesia), whereas in Africa a certain type of factionalism dominated policy-making and politics, retarding growth-enhancing economic diversification and infrastructural development.

When we come to the political economy of resource rents itself, Snyder and Bhavnani (2005) argue that the causal mechanism between rent-seeking

---

12. Although the Nigerian oil-rich Niger Delta is characterized by insurgencies, and there are ideological insurgencies led by the rebel group Boko Haram.

behaviour and resource rents may lie in a government *revenue* effect. This implies examining how the state obtains its revenues: whether or not taxing the mineral sector is important to the state. Even if a lootable sector exists it may not be as crucial to the state's coffers if other revenue sources exist side by side. Additionally, the mode of extraction matters: whether it is artisanal or industrial. Only the former makes resources lootable, as in Sierra Leone. Prior to 1985 its alluvial diamonds were extracted in an industrial fashion rather than by artisans, making it non-lootable. It did not collapse into civil war until after that. Finally, and most importantly, how governments spend their revenue matters: if the state spends its revenues on social welfare and growth-enhancing investment, conflict is less likely than if it appropriates revenues for factional and kleptocratic purposes. In Botswana, deep mineshaft diamonds, the security activities of the De Beers company and secure property rights made the diamonds largely uncontestable in terms of conflict.

Developed countries are considered largely immune to the resource curse, owing to their superior institutions of governance. Finland and Norway are two examples of successful European resource-rich countries, the first in its timber resources, the latter in oil. Finland's current economic success is not built on forestry but, rather, revolves around high-technology mobile telephony associated with Nokia. By contrast, in Norway oil continues to be the major export, and it does not have high-technology manufactured goods sectors comparable to those in Sweden and Finland. Consequently, a few signs of Dutch disease are discernible. The overall size of the public sector is not significantly different in Norway from that in neighbouring Sweden, however. Nevertheless, all Nordic countries that had resource-dependent economies at some point passed through transitions to fully fledged democracies and capitalist industrialization prior to any resource booms. They therefore avoided rent-seeking surges by special interest groups, which tend to occur in institutionally flawed situations, as pointed out by Torvik (2009). Another point is to do with the ownership of resource rents. In Norway the state not only has title to the country's oil wealth but has had command over 80 per cent of the resource rent since 1980. The revenue is invested in the Norwegian Petroleum Fund, akin to a trust fund for the benefit of current and future generations, but its full use is still impending. Such a policy yields a double dividend: it minimizes macroeconomic problems associated with boom and bust cycles and allows consumption-smoothing into the future, when resource revenues dry out.

Malaysia

Malaysia is deemed to be one of the successes among resource-abundant developing economies; see Auty and Gelb (2001), Zainal Abidin (2001) and Yusof (2011), for example. This is mainly because it achieved consistently high growth rates, and is now an upper middle-income economy. It is also cited as an example of a developing country with a major natural-resource-based sector, along with Indonesia, which managed to escape Dutch disease, in that it managed to *diversify* its economy and is a manufactured goods exporter. Finally, it has managed to maintain macroeconomic stability with overall fiscal prudence and a healthy savings rate, including a positive adjusted net savings ratio (explained below), as is the case with Botswana (Zainal Abidin 2001).

Malaysia's resource endowments are arguably more diverse than other resource-abundant economies, as they extend from cropland to forests and minerals and fuels. It has been a major exporter of rubber, tin, palm oil as well as petroleum.

At the time of the independence of Malaya in 1957, and the creation of the Malaysian Federation, the economy of Malaysia could be characterized as a rubber-exporting "tropical" stereotype, as described in Findlay and Lundahl (1999), with smallholder- rather than plantation-type agriculture prevailing. The interests of the smallholder indigenous (Bumiputera) agriculturists were paramount, as they constituted the support base for the largest segment in the governing coalitions.

At one time Malaysia could be viewed as among those resource-rich nations with a high risk of descending into ethnic conflict.[13] This is because of the ethnic cleavages between the majority indigenous people (Bumiputeras) and the Chinese, as well as Indian settlers. Serious race riots broke out in 1969, prompting the state to pursue greater affirmative action in favour of the majority, but poorer (compared to the Chinese), indigenous people. The economic side of these affirmative action policies, combined with serendipity and the country's geographical location within the world's most economically vibrant region of recent times (East Asia), aided the growth and economic achievements of Malaysia. Zainal Abidin (2001) argues that the

---

13.   There had been a Chinese-led communist insurgency in Malaya in the 1950s during British rule.

race riots of 1969, ethnic cleavages and the perceived need for affirmative action created the industrialization imperative, which in the Malaysian case is widely regarded to be successful. Not only that, Malaysia has also avoided outright civil war.

Commodity export instability constituted the earliest spur towards industrialization. As with other developing countries, an import substitution industrialization strategy was initially pursued in the 1960s (Zainal Abidin 2001; Yusof 2011). Following the 1969 riots the objective of industrialization was even more actively pursued under the New Economic Policy (NEP). In the early 1980s there was another industrial "big push", emphasizing certain heavy industrial sectors. Thereafter, policies for even more competitive industrialization were pursued. Many commentators (Zainal Abidin 2001 among them) regard Malaysia as one of the few examples of successful competitive industrialization emerging from resource abundance in the developing world. By "competitive industrialization" we mean manufacturing that is able to compete in international markets without (excessive) domestic protection. It is true that the present era of component trade, and the break-up of manufacturing production into many international locations, has allowed Malaysia to become a successful manufacturing goods exporter, in some cases of technologically sophisticated components. But one can be sceptical of the extent of domestic value added in manufacturing because of the large international trade in manufacturing components. Malaysia has been helped by its location in the East Asian manufacturing powerhouse of recent times, and its relative proximity to Japan, which engaged in active outward manufacturing investment in the post-1987 period. The Malaysian manufacturing base was, and is, heavily dependent on foreign direct investment (FDI), and this has led some commentators (such as Jomo 1990) to distinguish it from the Northeast Asian industrialization experiences of South Korea and Taiwan, where domestic, home-grown, entrepreneurship and research and development played a much more salient role.

Owing to its dependence on FDI, Malaysian trade policy was far more open than in many other developing countries, including resource-abundant economies bent on policies of diversification (Yusof 2011; Zainal Abidin 2001). What distinguishes Malaysia from most resource-rich economies is its positive net savings rates (equivalent to up to 15 per cent of GDP) and high gross domestic savings rates (above 35 per cent of GDP: Yusof 2011). It has also pursued prudent fiscal policies, maintained manageable government deficits and sound money, notwithstanding the Asian financial crisis of 1998. The real exchange rate was rarely overvalued and the economy mostly ran balance of payments surpluses (Yusof 2011). Thus, sound macro-management and open trade policies assisted the economy to diversify.

Malaysia is a major oil exporter, with most of its oil located in eastern Malaysia. Yusof (2011) outlines the activities of the Malaysian (now transnational) oil company Petronas. The management and taxation of oil revenues have been a success, according to Yusof (2011). Jomo and Hui (2003) describe the federal–state oil revenue split and other revenue-sharing mechanisms, and how they have to date avoided conflict and secessionist tendencies. There are calls for greater fiscal federalism, however, and for oil-producing states to receive a greater initial share of natural resource (mainly oil) revenues.

The undoubted success of Malaysia in avoiding Dutch disease is related to its strategy of diversification, aided by manufacturing FDI, a sound macroeconomic policy, including its high savings ratio, and the imperative of avoiding internal conflict.

Saudi Arabia

Saudi Arabia is the world's largest oil exporter, and as such a receiver of a very large oil rent. This has been characterized by volatility, as oil prices shoot up and down. There were upswings in oil prices twice in the 1970s and, more recently, in the first decade of the new millennium. Saudi Arabia is highly oil-dependent, and, in terms of resource dependence, its economy is one of the most reliant on oil in the world. This makes it the most typical example of a longstanding resource-dependent economy, and on a resource (oil) that is subject to one of the greatest volatilities in its price. According to an International Monetary Fund report (IMF 2015), the contribution of the oil sector to overall GDP was around 50 per cent in the 2005–7 period, albeit during an oil boom. Oil-sector-based revenues accounted for nearly 90 per cent of all government revenues. With the decline in oil prices in 2014 there was a sharp decline in economic growth, along with pressures on the public finances.

The volatility in its per capita income growth since the 1980s can be discerned from Figure 4.1, based on data from the World Bank's World Development Indicators database. Before that, high growth rates in the

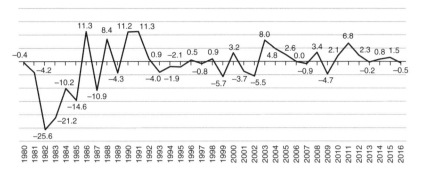

Figure 4.1 Per capita annual GDP growth rate in Saudi Arabia

1970s were achieved mainly as a result of a doubling of oil production, and oil revenues rose more than eightfold after 1973 (Auty 2001).

Auty (2001) argues that the state was able to control the oil rent as the production of oil had been nationalized, and, furthermore, the state appropriately taxed oil revenues, unlike in many other oil-rich states described in the "petromania" analysis of Karl (1999). Moreover, the state accumulated overseas assets based on the oil windfall. Thus, the worst-case scenario of the oil rents almost entirely falling into the hands of politically privileged private individuals was avoided. It set up development plans, which are discussed in detail in Ramady (2005). There was an emphasis on education and infrastructural development, which are growth-enhancing. The trade policy of the kingdom continued to remain open.

Auty (2001) points to several strategic errors in economic policy following the oil windfalls, however. Among them was an overestimation of the domestic economy's ability to absorb the increased income consequent to the oil windfall. This produced high rates of inflation in the 1970s. This would lead to real exchange rate appreciation. Second, the state has not diversified its taxation base beyond oil; this leads to the issues described by Ross (2001), when high oil rents lower executive accountability and democratic development. Third, market discipline was relaxed. This slowed down the process and pressures for economic diversification, despite the development plans. Highly protected and internationally uncompetitive agricultural and manufacturing sectors were encouraged; although, under the aegis of SABIC (Saudi Basic Industries Corporation), some success in petrochemicals has been achieved, the economy is still insufficiently diversified.

Above all, the classic Dutch disease phenomenon in terms of employment is an endemic characteristic of the Saudi economy. Saudi workers preferred jobs in government services, leaving other jobs, including in the traded sector, to foreign workers. Auty (2001) reports that 95 per cent of private sector jobs were in the hands of non-Saudis, whereas native Saudis worked for a bloated public sector enjoying generous salaries and benefits. This amounts to a transfer to the citizenry, funded by oil rents and government expenditure. Hence, the structure of the economy involved high government expenditure, including a transfer of the oil rent to ordinary citizens via the mechanism of public employment, which in the previous chapter was described in rent-seeking models, particularly those characterized by autocracy.

From the 1980s oil revenues declined, especially during various episodes: 1982–6, 1998–9, 2008–9, and again in 2014 (IMF 2015). The rent collapse was met, at least initially, by delayed fiscal adjustment. There was a tendency to draw down international reserves, cut capital government expenditure and reduce the number of foreign workers. The First Gulf War, in 1990–91, also put severe fiscal pressures on Saudi Arabia. Auty (2001) points out that, although government expenditure declined from 1982 to 1986, oil revenues fell more rapidly. It was only in 2004 that nominal oil revenues regained their 1982 peak (IMF 2015). During this period the government's exchange rate policy amounted to a real exchange rate appreciation. Subsidies to the domestic petrochemical industry were extensive.

After 2000, for about a decade, the non-oil sector grew at about 7 per cent per annum, creating 3.6 million jobs, although only about 20 per cent went to Saudi nationals (IMF 2015). Almost 70 per cent of Saudi nationals are employed in the public sector. The overall unemployment rate was estimated at 11.7 per cent in 2014 (IMF 2015),[14] but this figure is higher among the young and women and in certain regions. With a growing population, the problem of unemployment cannot be underestimated, particularly among women and the young. There are skill mismatches despite the huge investment in education. Total factor productivity was traditionally low, but has been growing since 2000. On the positive side, the extent of financial development is impressive, and the financial sector is reported by

---

14. The repatriation of foreign workers and a decline in outward remittances may cause real exchange rate appreciation.

the IMF (2015) to be in a healthy state, with sound macro-prudential regulation and adequately capitalized banks.

The most recent drop in oil prices, in 2014, has created fiscal challenges for the state. A recent report (IMF 2017b) indicates that the state has embarked on a reform process, however, in its attempts to reduce the non-oil primary fiscal deficit. This will require new sources of revenue, and further economic diversification. It remains to be seen whether growth in the non-oil sector (economic diversification), which began around 2000, and the nation's dependence on oil, which dates back eight decades, will be reduced under the state's ambitious "Vision 2030" plans. For a nation of over 30 million, with geo-strategic interests, the option of living on currently invested oil rents is much more limited than for some other highly oil-/gas-rich micro-states, such as Brunei.

Botswana

Botswana, a diamond-exporting economy, constitutes a rare successful case of consistent growth and development since the time of its independence. It is also regularly flagged up as one of the few resource-rich countries that have escaped the curse of natural resource dependence, and as an African success story.

At the time of its independence, in 1966, Botswana was one of the poorest nations in the world. According to Lewin (2011), nearly 60 per cent of the government's current expenditure was financed through development assistance. Since then it has achieved spectacular growth, with an annual average rise in per capita income of about 7 per cent between 1966 and 1999 (Lewin 2011), higher than that of three East Asian giants (Hong Kong, Singapore and South Korea). This has allowed it to achieve middle-income status, comparable to Mexico. Botswana has not only escaped the resource curse but has also avoided civil war, the other great risk afflicting resource-rich developing countries. Despite these successes, its economy, unlike in the case of Malaysia, has not diversified into manufacturing, and it is a highly unequal society, with Gini[15] coefficients of inequality hovering around 60

---

15. The Gini coefficient is the most commonly employed metric for inequality, particularly for measuring income inequality across households. It ranges from 0 to 100. A coefficient of 0 implies perfect equality across households, and 100 means that one individual household or group has all the income generated in an economy.

(IMF 2017a). Botswana's impressive achievements, within a neighbourhood principally characterized by failure, is usually explained through institutional factors and the adoption of good policies, although serendipity, as everywhere, has played a huge part.

According to Acemoglu, Johnson and Robinson (2003), the leading advocates of the institutional quality and growth nexus, the fact that Botswana has superior institutional quality[16] compared to other nations in sub-Saharan Africa is an analytical quandary. Given their thesis that good institutional quality was imbedded in countries where Europeans settled in substantial numbers, Botswana should clearly *not* have these. Consequently, Botswana's superior institutions are a statistical outlier, if their regressions about the quality of institutions being significantly and negatively related to settler mortality are to be believed. They argue that Botswana had good-quality and inclusive institutions in pre-colonial times. Tribal chiefs were used to widespread consultation, and there were constraints on their power. Second, the colonial experience was short, and the British colonial power did not tamper much with the pre-existing institutional infrastructure. The perpetuation of good institutional quality was in the economic interest of the post-independence elites, who were satisfied with rents from the diamond discovery and did not engage in excessive rent-seeking. They also argue that the decisions of President Seretse Khama and his successor, Quett Masire, imbued a strong and positive principle of agency over structure into the destiny of Botswana; see also Lewin (2011). Botswana is usually regarded to be the least corrupt African country by Transparency International.[17]

The views in Acemoglu, Johnson and Robinson (2003) are in contrast to those of Poteete (2009). She argues that the success of Botswana is based on stable and broad-based political coalitions, as well as the presence of external constraints, such as a currency that was tied to the rand, and having to deal with apartheid South Africa, including South Africa's trade policies. More generally, she argues that rent-seeking and wrong policies are more likely to emerge in more narrowly based and unstable coalitions. She

---

16. The major institution of importance centres on secure and widespread property rights.
17. See www.transparency.org/news/feature/corruption_perceptions_index_2017 (accessed 30 July 2018).

contests the Acemoglu, Johnson and Robinson (2003) contention that the pre-colonial institutions in Botswana necessarily promoted consensual politics and constraints on the executive. Poteete (2009) makes the important point that the emergence or non-emergence of the resource curse is not path-dependent on a country's initial institutional quality or set-up. Instead, the political coalition and institutional framework can alter, as we shall see in the case studies of Nigeria and Bolivia outlined below.

More important is the point that the country avoided serious rent-seeking contests that descend into civil war. As we shall see in the next chapter, one factor that may have come into play here is that Botswana's diamonds are Kimberlite deep mineshaft, making them physically less contestable. Diamond production began in Botswana in the early 1970s, shortly after independence. Production was based on an equal (50–50) partnership between the government and De Beers from South Africa. The country has been praised for sound fiscal management of these revenues. Instead of the windfall causing the usually public spending spree, a substantial amount of these rents were transferred into assets. Budgetary prudence was maintained, and Lewin (2011) points out that public sector saving was positive in every year from 1975 to 1996. Thus, government expenditure was delinked from revenues – no mean feat. In effect, the state sterilized the resource rents that would otherwise swell money supply via budget surpluses, as well as balance of payments surpluses (Lewin 2011).

Botswana, along with several neighbours, is a member of the South African Customs Union (SACU). This meant it eschewed import substitution industrialization policies with internationally uncompetitive parastatal enterprises. Botswana's currency is now pegged to the South African currency (the rand). Since the rand tends to depreciate against major currencies such as the dollar, Botswana's currency (the pula) has avoided real exchange rate appreciation.

Meijia and Castel (2012) discuss the Pula Fund, which is a sovereign wealth fund that aims to establish an inter-generational transfer of resource rents, as well as smooth consumption over the fluctuating revenue cycle. It has to be said that diamond revenues are considerably smoother than oil revenues. The Pula Fund had assets valued at US$7 billion in 2008, and is subdivided between an investment account, with consumption smoothing in mind, and an inter-generational equity fund. In addition to the Pula Fund the central bank also maintains a portfolio of liquid assets.

Despite these successes, growth has slowed during the new millennium. Diamond resources are due to be depleted. The diamond industry is highly capital-intensive, and consequently a serious problem of unemployment exists (IMF 2017a). Moreover, despite the presence of development plans, the country has failed to truly diversify into a manufacturing exporter like Malaysia. Thus, the growth-sustaining structural transformation (Rodrik 2016) has not taken place. The country is also characterized by very high inequality, which ultimately destabilizes society. Its greatest achievement is, perhaps, the fact that the country's very substantial resource rents did not lead to civil war, as has been the case in many nations in its neighbourhood.

Nigeria

Nigeria is the African continent's most populous nation, with about 186 million inhabitants (World Development Indicators). Table 1.2, in Chapter 1, prominently features Nigeria in the list of growth failures at around the turn of the millennium. According to Ajakaiye, Collier and Ekpo (2011), the growth in nominal GDP was an annual average of only 1.9 per cent between 1970 and 2003. This was below population growth, making Nigeria a growth failure. Growth did pick up during the commodity boom of the last decade, but it collapsed again in 2016. Nigeria is rich in minerals and fuels, and is one of the world's largest oil exporters. According to the World Bank's World Development Indicators, its per capita income still makes it a lower middle-income country; see Figure 4.2, which illustrates the evolution of GDP per capita growth in Nigeria. When utilizing the globally comparable absolute poverty measure of US$1.90 per day in 2011 purchasing power parity terms, a staggering 53.5 per cent of the population lived below this international poverty line (World Development Indicators). The country is heavily dependent on oil exports, and oil revenues constitute the major source of fiscal revenue in the country. Nigeria, therefore, is a case of the resource curse par excellence, to which the various theories of rent-seeking (manifesting itself in corruption) can be applied.

Oil was first discovered in Nigeria in 1956. The Biafran civil war in the late 1960s was not unrelated to oil rents. The prospecting and exploitation rights were granted to foreign companies, and later a national oil company was also established. Additionally, joint ventures were also set up, and

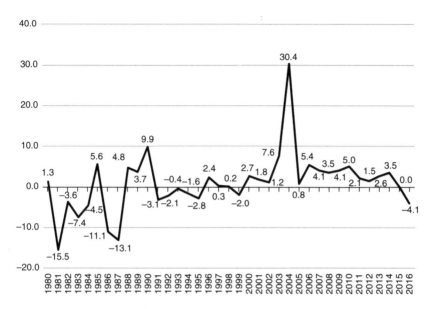

Figure 4.2 Per capita annual GDP growth rate in Nigeria

the Nigerian state did try and compel foreign companies to transfer technical know-how to Nigerian nationals. Despite these measures, inadequate domestic capacity to run the oil industry characterizes Nigeria (Ajakaiye, Collier & Ekpo 2011), with crucial operating decisions still resting with foreign petroleum firms. The oil-producing region in the Niger Delta has been subjected to serious environmental degradation, with its once vibrant agro-forestry sector greatly compromised. Notwithstanding its oil wealth, the region continues to be one of the most deprived regions of the country. In the 1990s armed conflict broke out between the local (Ogoni) people and the oil companies. The Nigerian military was drawn into the conflict, and by 2009 an amnesty for insurgents was announced, as well as guarantees of direct transfers of 10 per cent of oil revenues. Many of the promises remain unfulfilled, and the region remains at risk of conflict.

Ajakaiye, Collier and Ekpo (2011) point out that the petroleum profit taxes and royalty rates were set at appropriate levels, and gradually rose over time. Much more concerning is the economy's huge dependence on oil taxes as the single and overwhelming source of fiscal revenue for the state; it has never been below 70 per cent of total revenues. Not only has this exposed government revenues to the volatility in oil prices, but it is also indicative of a low tax base and the failure to diversify sources of revenue. Another implication of this dependence is that the state's fiscal balances shadow the boom–bust cycles in oil prices, one of the most volatile of all commodity prices.

Nigeria has also been subjected to major Dutch disease effects, which have crowded out its tradable sector. A once vibrant, diversified agricultural and fisheries sector that produced for export was rendered uncompetitive. In addition, a nascent manufacturing sector that produced for domestic consumption, as well as for neighbouring countries, was crowded out; see Ajakaiye, Collier and Ekpo (2011), who also indicate episodes of real exchange rate appreciation. This was also pointed out earlier by Pinto (1987), who contrasts oil-exporting Indonesia with Nigeria. The real exchange rate was allowed to appreciate in Nigeria, whereas this was not permitted in Indonesia; agriculture did not decline in Indonesia, thanks to deliberate policies; and foreign borrowing was much more constrained in Indonesia compared to Nigeria.

One of the major policy failings of the management of oil revenues in Nigeria was the absence of precautionary saving behaviour or saving to offset the depletion of this non-renewable resource in Nigeria during the oil booms of the 1970s. Instead of saving or asset accumulation, large external debts were built up, fuelled by corruption and capital flight. General Abacha is claimed to have amassed US$4 billion abroad during his tenure as Nigeria's head of state (Ajakaiye, Collier & Ekpo 2011). Nigeria has frequently topped the list of the most corrupt countries in the global Corruption Perceptions Index of Transparency International.[18]

A great deal of public domestic investment was of the "white elephant" variety theorized in Robinson and Torvik (2005). For example, the construction of the new capital in Abuja was characterized by unfinished buildings. Salisu (2000) attempts to gauge the extent of corruption in Nigeria via the indirect method of estimating the shadow economy. Not surprisingly, he finds a considerable negative effect of this proxy on growth, but also a negative effect of investment on growth, suggesting that corruption detracts

---

18. Just as Botswana is regarded as the least corrupt African nation; see www.transparency. org/news/feature/corruption_perceptions_index_2017 (accessed 27 July 2018).

from the quality of investment, as in the theoretical model outlined in Appendix 1.

In many ways, several theoretical propositions outlined in Chapter 3 are borne out in the Nigerian case. First of all, we have an application of the voracity effect theorized by Lane and Tornell (1996). We have a case of oil retarding democratic development, as argued by Ross (2001), and democratic accountability (Collier & Hoeffler 2009). In addition, the white elephant theory of inefficient public projects (Robinson & Torvik 2005) is applicable. The behaviour of the political elites, particularly during military regimes, is reminiscent of the rent-seeking, repression and authoritarianism described in Caselli and Cunningham (2007) and Caselli and Tesei (2016). The idea is that, faced with a choice between developmental and rent-seeking policies, the leadership veered towards authoritarianism and increased rent-seeking, unlike in the case of Botswana outlined above.

All this changed with the advent of President Obasanjo in 1999, when a more developmental role on the part of the state gradually emerged (Ajakaiye, Collier & Ekpo 2011). Not only did growth increase (see Figure 4.2) but stabilization funds to save oil revenues were set up (the excess crude fund), the country paid off a great deal of its international debt and Nigeria became an active member of the Extractive Industries Transparency Initiative (EITI), publishing information on resource revenues paid not just to the Nigerian federal government but also to its constituent states. All this was achieved during a period of favourable and high oil prices; whether Nigeria's return to good fortune can be sustained during a period of falling oil prices remains to be seen.

Chile

Chile is a longstanding upper middle-income economy, according to the widely utilized World Bank classification of living standards in the world's economies. It is also extremely rich in a variety of natural resources, and is the biggest player in the world market for copper, accounting for 43 per cent of the world's copper exports (Fuentes 2011). Its economic record suggests that it is a successful resource-rich country that has diversified its economy like Malaysia (thereby reducing resource dependence). It has also reduced its fiscal dependence on resource rents, and adopted legally binding fiscal

rules that constrain the annual budgetary stance of the state, as well as operating a variety of stabilization funds related to resource rents.

Prior to the infamous military coup of 1973, which brought General
Pinochet to power, the economy of Chile had more than a light touch of
state intervention. The government operated a large number of state-owned
enterprises and copper accounted for 75 per cent of Chile's exports and 30
per cent of government revenues, with the budget deficit at around 12 per
cent of national income, along with high inflation and widespread financial repression (Fuentes 2011). In 1971 several large copper mines were
nationalized by the state without much compensation forthcoming to the
former owners. Following the coup of 1973, Chilean economic policies were
governed by what was then known as "monetarism", which in contemporary
parlance can be characterized by the term "neoliberal". This meant widespread privatization, the pursuit of fiscal prudence, low inflation targets
and, above all, a more open international trade regime. The pursuit of trade
openness may have been a necessary precondition that helped to diversify
the country's export structure.

It has to be pointed out that the real per capita growth rate of the Chilean
economy was one of the few that was positive in Latin America during the
infamous lost decade of the 1980s. After the end of the dictatorship, in 1989,
the country reverted to democracy. A political consensus emerged, however, and meant that market discipline and an outward economic orientation were maintained. Thus, rent-seeking was curtailed. Above all, the
sanctity of property rights was maintained, and the risk of appropriation
minimized (Fuentes 2011).

There is a large state-owned copper-mining firm, CODELCO, which is
the largest producer, but its share of total production has declined over time
to about 20 per cent by 2010 (Fuentes 2011). The country has been very
successful in attracting inward investment (FDI) into the copper-mining
sector, particularly in the post-1995 period. This is, no doubt, down to the
high regard for institutional quality in Chile, particularly related to property
rights. There is also a flat tax applied (for ten years) to the taxable income
of foreign investors, the period of which is extended for larger investors.
There is little doubt that an open trade regime and high institutional quality
facilitated this process.

The country has managed to avoid Dutch disease and successfully
diversified its exports. Whereas mining output accounted for 85.5 per

cent of the country's exports in 1970, its share declined to 58.7 per cent in 2008, even during a commodity and copper price boom. Meanwhile, the share of manufactured exports rose from 11.6 to 35.3 per cent during the same period (Fuentes 2011). A sizeable share of the manufactured exports are from processed natural resource products; in that way resource abundance did not contribute to growth failure (Murshed & Serino 2011). The country's Herfindahl index of export concentration, which takes the maximum value of 1 if one export item accounts for 100 per cent of total exports, has been steady at 0.1 since the mid-1980s (Fuentes 2011). An econometric study of the spillovers from mining to the other sectors of the economy by Pérez Ruiz (2017) suggests strong positive spillovers from mining or commodity price booms to both the traded and non-traded sectors in Chile. There is a positive wealth response for the economy due to forward linkages to the demand for goods and services, and backward linkages to the demand for intermediate inputs. The positive stimulus of a copper price boom to manufacturing (the traded sector) is greater than for construction (the non-traded sector).

Chile has avoided overdependence on resource rents, and has diversified its tax base. Resource- or copper-based taxes accounted for 16.4 per cent of government revenues around 2010, similar to that in 1990, but lower than in the pre-1973 period. In the post-1973 era a fiscal surplus has been continually maintained (Fuentes 2011). In recent years revenues from copper royalties have been financing a fund for innovation and competitiveness, administered by the Ministry of Economic Affairs with a view to doubling per capita income by 2020. In addition, there are two sovereign wealth funds in which resource rent are invested. The first is the Economic and Social Stabilization Fund (ESSF), which is meant to accumulate assets during periods of high prices. This was formerly the copper stabilization fund. Its aim is to smooth government spending around the commodity price cycle. Its assets amounted to about 11 per cent of GDP in late 2008 (Fuentes 2011). The second sovereign wealth fund is the Pension Reserve Fund (PRF). This assists in maintaining inter-generational equity, and by legislation the fund must increase by between 0.2 and 0.5 per cent of GDP per annum, with accumulated assets equivalent to around 1.5 per cent of GDP in 2008. Both these sovereign wealth funds are run by the Central Bank of Chile.

Of great interest is the fiscal rule governing the government's budgetary stance, a measure introduced in 2001; see Fuentes (2011) and

Schmidt-Hebbel (2012) for details. Under this rule, all variables are cyclically adjusted over the trend in the business cycle and commodity (copper) prices. Current government expenditure is given by the difference between cyclically adjusted revenues less the cyclically adjusted central government balance. The estimation of the trend and long-term figures for revenue are a matter for estimation, as they are non-observable. These are carried out by two advisory councils. In following the rule, Chile is helped by the fact that it has few automatic stabilizers: expenditures and transfers that increase during downswings in the business cycle. Schmidt-Hebbel (2012) argues that the rule lowers pro-cyclical biases in fiscal policy, which are characteristic of many resource-dependent economies, and greatly augments fiscal policy credibility.

Bolivia

Bolivia, a landlocked lower middle-income economy in Latin America, has a long history in mining, harking back to the "Atlantic" economy and the first epoch of globalization (Findlay & Lundahl 1999) between 1870 and 1914. Its mineral wealth consists of hard minerals – tin, zinc, silver and gold – as well as hydrocarbons more recently. It is also ethnically fractionalized, with a substantial indigenous population, who are traditionally marginalized. The Bolivian economy was characterized by the growth collapse which occurred in many parts of Latin America in the 1980s, followed by a recovery, especially during the most recent experience of the commodity price boom. But its economy has had a chequered history, and it cannot, despite recent successes, be characterized as a case of a resource-rich economy that escaped the resource curse. One of the characteristics of the Bolivian economy is the fact that it has been landlocked since 1883, and, given the terrain, transport costs are very high. In what follows I will focus closely on the failure to manage resource rents in the 1973–85 period, rather than dwelling on recent successes in lowering poverty and addressing structural inequality.

Following a political upheaval in 1952, the Bolivian economy became increasingly state-led, as was the case worldwide during that time. Compared to many countries in Latin America, its human development indicators were more disadvantaged. For example, life expectancy at birth in the early

1970s was 46, compared to Mexico's 62; but this has to be understood in the context of the high inequality in Latin America. As is to be expected, many of the mines were nationalized following the events of 1952. But, as Auty and Evia (2001) point out, it led to a decline in the mining sector. The resources extracted from the mining sector went to the state but were inefficiently invested. Bolivia, like many countries at the time, followed an import substitution industrialization strategy, and it is claimed that public investment during that time was inefficient (Auty & Evia 2001).

The commodity and oil price booms of the 1970s provided the Bolivian state with a huge increase in natural resource rents. According to Auty and Evia (2001), the national income share of mineral rents went up from 6.5 per cent in 1973 to 25.5 per cent by 1982. These rents were mismanaged, as in all countries that permitted themselves to be subject to a resource curse, such as Nigeria. The government failed to save the increase in resource rents, or to utilize it to retire pre-existing public debt. Not only that, but further debt was accumulated, and current account deficits in the balance of payments were recorded. By 1984 the debt/GDP ratio was 116 per cent and debt servicing as a proportion of exports was 49 per cent. Bolivia had landed well and truly into the infamous Latin American debt crisis of the 1980s, which was at least partially, if not chiefly, responsible for what is now labelled as the "lost decade" of the 1980s for that region. By 1984 Bolivia was insolvent, being compelled to limit debt servicing to a quarter of export earnings (Auty & Evia 2001). Additionally, there was unsustainable financing of budget deficits via money creation, leading to hyperinflation; the Bolivian inflation rate accelerated to some 20,000 per cent by 1985.

On the real side of the economy, the resource rent windfall led to the classic Dutch disease outcome: deindustrialization. Given that Bolivia is landlocked and mountainous, making transportation difficult and expensive, its traded consumer manufacturing sector is per se non-traded or more readily competitive with imported manufactures. But real exchange rate appreciation was permitted, and the domestic manufacturing sector was consequently rendered uncompetitive compared to imported substitutes.

The debt crisis, hyperinflation, the decline in commodity prices and the ethnically based structural inequality in Bolivian society (Auty & Evia 2001) forced a change in economic policy, accompanied, as is common, by political change. Growth started to pick up (Figure 4.3), and, with the exception

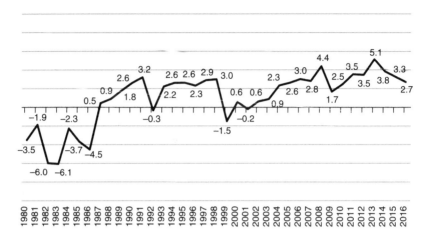

Figure 4.3 Per capita annual GDP growth rate in Bolivia

of a dip around the start of the millennium, increases in per capita income have been positive.

Not only has the country made impressive strides in reducing poverty; Toscani (2017) points out, that based on censuses of the population in 2001 and 2012, the poverty head count declined from 58.6 per cent to 44.9 per cent on the basis of national poverty lines. The more recent boom has not retarded growth but increased growth with equity, as has been well publicized (Cornia 2014). Toscani (2017) estimates that the natural resource boom of the last decade lowered poverty by 3 per cent more in Bolivian municipalities that were mineral-producing.

The Bolivian hydrocarbon industry was renationalized in 2006 by President Morales. This has raised the share of rents going to the public sector, and there has been a greater focus on poverty reduction (OECD 2017). Among other measures, there was a new law imposing a direct tax on hydrocarbons of 32 per cent. Some of the revenues were earmarked for poverty reduction, such as Renta Dignidad (a pension scheme) and Bono Juancito Pino (a conditional cash transfer for school-aged children); see OECD (2017). These recent measures have helped Bolivia achieve growth with redistribution and poverty reduction; see Mosley (2017: chap. 5) for more details.

The cross-country econometric evidence for the resource curse is very mixed. Even if one accepts the artificial distinction between the economic resource curse (mainly on growth, but also on other economic variables such as education expenditure) and the political resource curse (on governance, chiefly corruption and democracy/autocracy), the picture continues to be mixed. There is greater evidence for a resource curse in operation when one considers the 1970s and 1980s, and in the earlier more cross-sectional econometric analyses. The application of panel data methods results in more ambiguous findings. There is, for example, a continuing and lively controversy as to whether oil dependence dampens democratic development. Evidence for the institutional resource curse becomes weaker after 2000, as does the negative effect of resource rents on growth. Studies on the subnational resource curse come up with more consensual results, pointing to the presence of a resource curse for natural-resource-rich regions, except when it comes to studies comparing the different states of the United States.

One must remember, however, that cross-country econometrics gives us *average* outcomes, and the results do tend to vary depending on the technique applied and the period of coverage. At the moment it would appear that greater sophistication in econometric techniques diminishes the probability of finding evidence for the resource curse at the cross-country level. Regression coefficients, or the average outcomes just alluded to, are not universal findings! That is why the case study method can be more informative, as – unlike, say, the Newtonian physical laws of motion – there are no universal laws governing the existence or absence of the resource curse, except if one believes in path dependence. Path dependence suggests that the initial post-discovery political environment, as well as institutional quality, will determine whether a nation will be afflicted by the resource curse or not (as exemplified in the widely cited paper by Mehlum, Moene and Torvik 2006). The six cases studies presented above, however, point to a mixed bag of outcomes, as I outline three instances of countries avoiding the curse, as well as three cases of being subject to the curse. Even then, the cases of Bolivia and Nigeria suggest that, although these countries were initially afflicted by a resource curse, they eventually managed to escape it as the political and institutional environment changed to a more "pro-indiginesta" policy and a civilian administration respectively. This suggests that the path-dependent methodology of cross-sectional and cross-country econometric could yield flawed evidence (see Mehlum, Moene & Torvik 2006; and Isham *et al.* 2005, for example).

What are the lessons to be derived from those countries that have successfully avoided the resource curse? They pursued cautious counter-cyclical fiscal policies (the best example is Chile, with its fiscal rules), avoided real exchange rate appreciation, set up precautionary funds and successfully avoided overdependence on natural resources by undergoing structural transformation of their production structures (perhaps not in Botswana). I shall examine these factors (except for structural change and industrialization, dealt with in Chapter 2) in Chapter 6. But, before that, I wish to analyse how natural resource rents contributes to the risk of civil war.

5

Resource rents and violent internal conflict

Resource rents, particularly of the point-sourced variety, were widely regarded to be a major factor contributing towards the risk of civil war in developing countries, following the influential work of Collier and Hoeffler (2004).[1] According to this view, conflict reflects elite competition over valuable point-sourced natural resource rents, and this is when the rent-seeking contests associated with the presence of resource rents in weak institutional settings, which we reviewed in Chapter 3, descend into outright warfare. Fearon and Laitin (2003) argue that civil war risk is mainly attributable to diminished state capacity: the inability of the state to either provide public services or suppress rebellion in weak and failing polities with weak institutions that are also characterized by low incomes. Resource rents should augment the state's resources, but not always when there is large-scale rent-seeking by powerful actors.

There is a longstanding position, however, that relative deprivation (Gurr 1970) and the *grievance* that it produces fuel internal violence. Identity can be crucial to grievance mobilization. This is due to the collective action problem, as discussed in Olson (1965). Ethnic identities, whether based on race, language, religion, tribal affiliation or regional differences, may serve as a more effective amalgam for the purposes of group formation, compared to other forms of more transient difference, such as socio-economic class. The formation of enduring identities is therefore central to mobilizing groups; see Tilly (1978) on this.[2] Large-scale conflict between groups cannot

---

1. This chapter draws upon my previous work on this topic, including Murshed (2010: chap. 3).
2. Tilly (1978) argues that grievances or relative deprivation (Gurr 1970) are insufficient to engender rebellion. Rebellion requires mass or group mobilization, needing resources and a weakened or failing state, as well as the development of a narrative of disadvantage and discrimination.

proceed without the presence of palpably perceived group differences, or grievances, which may have historical dimensions. More recently, Stewart (2000) has introduced the notion of *horizontal inequality*, the inequality between groups, rather than the inequality that may exist between individual households in an otherwise ethnically homogeneous population (vertical inequality). In this connection, it has to be borne in mind that resource rents may become a source of grievance, if they are distributed unequally, or if certain groups are excluded from the benefits of the resource rents, particularly in resource-producing regions.

This chapter reviews how the presence of natural resource rents can encourage internal conflict, usually taking the form of civil war. I first consider theoretical aspects, followed by a survey of the empirical evidence. As we shall see, no consensus emerges in the literature when we come to the cross-country evidence; individual case studies point to the saliency of resource rents, if mismanaged, as a potential source of grievance that can turn into armed conflict.

Resource rents and internal conflict: theory

In Collier and Hoeffler (2004), civil wars stem from the greedy behaviour of a rebel group in organizing an insurgency against the government. Greed is about the opportunities faced by the rebel group. The opportunities can be disaggregated into three components: financing, recruitment and geography. The most common sources of rebel finance are the appropriation of natural resources, donations from sympathetic diasporas residing abroad and contributions either from foreign states hostile to the government or from multinational companies interested in the region. Natural resource wealth is the chief among the three in terms of its relative importance. Recruitment is about the opportunity to induct fighting manpower; something made easier when there is a high proportion of young unemployed males in the population, in a setting of endemic poverty and poor education. Geographical situations favourable to rebel groups are mountainous terrain and other safe havens for insurgents. In short, greed simply measures the economic returns from fighting, and should be distinguished from sociopolitical grievances.

Collier and Hoeffler's (2004) empirical findings conclude that the set of variables representing rebel opportunity or greed akin to loot-seeking are the main reasons for civil war. By implication, the alternative hypothesis of grievance (justice-seeking), focusing on ethnic religious divisions, political repression and horizontal inequality, is dismissed, although its invalidity is not formally tested for. Natural resource rents constitute "booty", and this fact has been used to emphasize the greed or *criminal* motivation for civil war. Central to Collier and Hoeffler's (2004) empirical testing for the greed hypothesis is the role of primary commodities in the economic structure. They measure the dependence on natural resources by the share of primary commodity exports in GDP, and the validity of this metric, as well as the statistical robustness of the relationship between resource rents and the risk of conflict, has been called into question.

If economic agents (*Homo economicus*) are actuated mainly by self-interest, we must demonstrate why they choose war over other alternatives. Therefore, any theorizing about greed must be based on the economic motivations for violence and criminality. Belligerents in the wars of natural-resource-rich countries could be acting in ways closer to what Olson (1996) refers to as "roving bandits" – who have no encompassing interest in preserving the state or its people but are simply intent on loot – than to "stationary" bandits, who take control of the state and seek to maximize their own profit by encouraging stability and growth in their new domain. Civil wars motivated by the desire to control natural resource rents could also mirror "warlord competition", a term that owes its origins to the violent competition between leaders attempting to control economic resources in the context of medieval Europe (Skaperdas 2002).

A proper greed-based theory of civil war must relate to the trade-off between production and predation in making a living, whereby we may view war as theft writ large. Violence is one means of appropriating the resources of others. Note that armed conflict implies the absence of contractual or consensual interaction (see Edgeworth 1881), which is in stark contrast to the alternative method of benefiting from the endowments of others via peaceful and voluntary exchange (trade) between economic agents, groups or nations. This implies that we also need to specify the conditions under which violence becomes a viable or more attractive option relative to other alternatives.

A variety of game-theoretic models exist that describe the non-cooperative and conflictive interaction between groups, in which the object is to capture the rival's endowment by force.[3] One such model is Hirshleifer's (1995), in which each group has a fixed resource endowment, which can be used to produce either goods for consumption or armaments to fight the other group. Groups exist in a state of non-contractual anarchy *vis-à-vis* each other; this also implies the absence of enforceable property rights. The object of fighting is to capture some of the rival's endowment. Success in war is uncertain, and the probability of victory is given by a Tullock (1967) contest success function, in which the probability of victory for any one group is given by its own military expenditure relative to the total fighting outlay made by all sides. Additionally, there is a military effectiveness parameter, akin to what is known as a force multiplier in military establishments: something that raises the effectiveness of each unit of fighting effort. In the absence of increasing returns to scale in military effectiveness, and if a minimum subsistence income is present, there will be a Nash non-cooperative equilibrium associated with some fighting. In other words, in the equilibrium, both (or all) parties will be engaged in some fighting with each other, as well as some productive activities, unless one side manages to vanquish others thanks to its military superiority.

Hirshleifer (1995) describes this as a state of anarchy – something akin to primitive tribal warfare. Furthermore, anarchy implies the complete absence of a social contract between different groups, in contrast to the attributes of a functioning modern nation state. Note, also, that no possibility of inter-group trade is permitted.

Skaperdas (1992) outlines a model that is similar because it has a fixed resource endowment, which can be devoted to either production or armament. The probability of success in war also depends on a similar contest success function. Skaperdas (1992) allows for a peaceful trading cooperative equilibrium, however, when there is no fighting. The parties simply share the sum of total resources in proportion to the contest success function, or in accordance with what would have been the equilibrium outcome of war. This is likely when the probability of military success for either side is low, and both parties are similar in their peaceful productive capacities.

---

3. In Chapter 3 I reviewed models related to pure rent-seeking. In this chapter I look only at models that include violent conflict, and try to avoid overlap with Chapter 3.

Second, there is a possible outcome in which one side only produces, whereas the other party does some fighting and production. This is a more likely outcome when the more pacific side is more productive, and the side that chooses fighting is more efficient at it. Finally, both sides may choose a mix of fighting and production. As with the first possibility, each side must be similar in its economic productivity and fighting effectiveness, but here the technology of war is such that it raises the probability of victory for both sides; hence the presence of fighting. In many ways, Skaperdas's (1992) model puts the trade-off between fighting and predation into sharper perspective, and explicitly mentions the absence of contract or respect for property rights.

Both these models neglect the destructiveness of war (collateral damage), however, and its capacity to ravage productive capacity, in addition to the direct military expenditure. These models employ intermediate inputs, and not factors of production, which can be costlessly shifted between fighting and production. Second, there is no growth in these models, something that would raise the opportunity costs of war. A similar effect could arise from complementarities in production between groups and/or economies of scale, which would lead to mergers between groups or cooperation in each faction's self-interest. Third, the possibilities of peaceful exchange need to be limited (they are absent in Hirshleifer 1995) in order to rationalize conflict. In traditional economics the gains from trade arise mainly from differences in tastes, technology and endowments, and these gains from trade need to be minimized in order to make conflict an optimal choice. Violent means are attractive when the intention is to extract resources (as in the case of colonial plantations and mines and in societies associated with increased voracity for rent-seeking) or accumulate surpluses at the expense of others (mercantilism). Fourth, these models imply full information. In the presence of asymmetric information, misperceptions about contest success, the opposition's intentions, and so on, wars that do not maximize expected utility under full information may break out, akin to problems associated with moral hazard and adverse selection.

On another note, taking into account external shocks, Dal Bó and Dal Bó (2011) outline a three-sector model of the economy consisting of two productive sectors (one capital and the other labour-intensive) and a predation sector involving rent contests. A fall in the relative return to labour encourages predation, and possibly conflict. This can happen if an external shock raises the relative return to capital, as is possible during a resource boom.

By contrast, identity and group formation are central to grievance-based theories of conflict. An individual's utility may be related to his identity, specifically the relative position of the group he identifies with in the social pecking order; see Akerlof and Kranton (2000). An individual may derive utility from certain normative forms of behaviour appropriate to his identity but considered deviant by other groups, and may even face sanctions from like-minded group members if he deviates from them. This type of behavioural paradigm may be related to solving the collective action problems (Olson 1965), without which organized large-scale violence is impossible, even if we believe conflict is primarily motivated by greed.

The notion of relative deprivation dates back to the work of Gurr (1970), who defines it as the discrepancy between what people think they deserve and what they actually believe they can get; in short, the disparity between aspirations and achievements. It also needs to be distinguished from a state of absolute deprivation, which occurs in situations characterized by endemic poverty. In these situations, no group may feel relatively deprived, and the forces of rebellion may be more muted. Relative deprivation is more likely to arise when the situation is improving for some, and not for others. It is the difference between what "ought" to be and what actually "is", according to Gurr (1970).

Tilly's (1978) mobilization theory is a critique of relative deprivation. He argues that grievances are ubiquitous, and for grievances to transform themselves into rebellion (or conflict) resources have to be mobilized, and a timely challenge has to be mounted against the state or the incumbents in power at a time of their relative weakness. Even so, relative deprivation can be considered to be a major cause of civil war, as well as sectarian and routine violence, since it can stimulate general frustration or be used by conflict entrepreneurs as a unifying tool or as a means for group mobilization for collective action.

The notion of *horizontal* inequalities between groups, classified by ethnicity, religion, linguistic differences, tribal affiliations, etc., is thought to be an important cause of contemporary civil war and sectarian strife. The expression "horizontal inequality" originates in the work of Stewart (see Stewart 2000), and should be distinguished from *vertical* inequality, which is the inequality within an otherwise homogeneous population. Vertical inequality, say in income or wealth, is the economic inequality that exists across individual households within a group assumed to be culturally homogeneous. It is also the most commonly measured type of inequality. The well-known Gini and Theil measures of income inequality, say within a nation state, define inequality across economic groups that differ from each other in one aspect only, income, but are otherwise assumed homogeneous.

Horizontal inequality aims to measure inequality across groups based on an ethnic group identity, such as between Catholics *vis-à-vis* Protestants, Hutus relative to Tutsis, and so on. Note that, within each group relevant to horizontal inequality, there will be rich and poor individuals or households. So, for example, if we are considering the Catholic–Protestant divide, within both Catholic and Protestant groups there are some rich and poor individuals and households. What really matters are the differences between the two groups, not the within-group inequalities in each of these individual identities. As far as vertical inequality is concerned, within-group inequalities are often as important as between-group differences in decomposing changes in overall inequality between different time periods. It has to be remembered, however, that vertical inequality pertains to the individual or household as the unit of measurement. Thus, the differences between horizontal and vertical inequality mainly pertain to *group* definition, and groups can be classified in many ways (ethnicity, language, religion, and so on). Four sources of horizontal inequality may be highlighted.

First, *discrimination in public spending and taxation*. Discrimination in the allocation of public spending and unfair tax burdens lead to serious unrest. Grossman (1991) has developed a theoretical model of insurrection against the state by the peasantry reacting to overtaxation, when the state is a tax farmer interested in maximizing the income of the rentier class. A peasant farmer household has a choice between agricultural production, soldiering for the state or engaging in rebellion against the state. A lot depends on the probability of the success of rebellion. If this is substantial, along with a high enough tax rate on peasant output, rebellion occurs. Even though rebellion reduces overall production and average income, it can increase the expected income of the peasantry. The presence of capturable resource rents can raise the value of rebellion to the oppressed, as well as increasing potential returns to repression for those in power.

Second, *high asset inequality*. Agrarian societies with high inequality – for example, El Salvador, Guatemala, Nepal, the Philippines and

Zimbabwe – have high asset inequality, and are very prone to conflict. Asset redistribution, such as land reform to lessen inequality, is more difficult than public finance reform.

Third, *economic mismanagement and recession*. In Africa, Latin America and the former Soviet Union, conflict-ridden countries have also suffered prolonged economic mismanagement and growth collapse. Successive IMF- and World-Bank-supported adjustment programmes in DRC/Zaire, Somalia and elsewhere not only proved incapable of promoting economic recovery but, given the level of corruption within the state, became targets for capture by elite groups. Economic mismanagement is often associated with an uneven and unfair distribution of the burdens of subsequent adjustment; public spending benefiting the elite and the military is protected, often favouring particular ethnic groups, with the burden of adjustment placed on expenditures of value to the poor and disadvantaged groups. Moreover, as Rodrik (1999) emphasizes, countries with weak institutions of conflict management as well as high income inequality are less able to withstand economic shocks and experience growth failure. They are also more prone to the risk of civil strife and war, since their weak institutions, which are further weakened by shocks and lower growth, are unable to withstand the resulting social pressure and distributional conflict. Many resource-rich economies are subject to the resource curse, and have been mismanaged, as seen in the last two chapters. This adds to conflict risk.

Fourth, *grievances related to resource rents*. Natural resource rents can in themselves become a serious source of grievance, if local populations feel that they are not getting a fair share of these, as many subnational studies illustrate. This phenomenon is perhaps the most important conflict-producing channel when there are resource rents. It can lead to secessionist wars, calls for greater autonomy and fiscal federalism. For example, in Nigeria, in more than seven years of civilian rule, the state at all levels (local, state and federal) is perceived to have failed to bring tangible economic benefits for impoverished local residents of the Niger Delta. Even Nigeria's federal system indirectly encourages violence in the delta by rewarding those who pose the greatest threats to oil facilities with lucrative oil contracts and government positions (ICG 2006). It can also cause secessionist tendencies among relatively rich regions that no longer want to subsidize their fellow countrymen, as in the case of Aceh and Papua in Indonesia. During three decades of the relatively stable authoritarian regime of Suharto, rents from these natural-resource-rich provinces were used to achieve equitable social development across the country, which was beneficial from a national point of view, but created grievances in the wealth-producing regions. After the regime collapsed in 1998, such a policy could not be continued, and new schemes of revenue-sharing were introduced under special autonomy settings in both provinces (see Tadjoeddin 2014).

Empirical evidence on resource rents and civil war

While Collier and Hoeffler (2004) press the greedy rebel hypothesis derived from their findings regarding the strong explanatory power of the share of primary commodity exports to GDP (their proxy for natural resource wealth), others are less sanguine. In short, the empirical controversy over the link between natural resource wealth and greed hypothesis is about the saliency of measurement issues, the problem of reverse causality and possible mechanisms in between natural resource rents and conflict. On the matter of measurement, two broad sets of issues need to be considered: (a) the measure of natural resource wealth/abundance and resource dependence and (b) the construction of the relevant conflict dependent variable.

Before we examine the various alternative metrics for natural resource dependence, note that the term "primary commodity" includes both agricultural commodities and minerals/fuels but, crucially, excludes illegal substances (coca and heroin) as well as illicit alluvial diamonds in Collier and Hoeffler (2004). Certain varieties of resources are more easily captured: they may be lootable, such as alluvial diamonds (in Sierra Leone, Angola) available along riverbeds using artisanal techniques, or illicit drugs, such as coca in Colombia; or obstructable, such as an oil pipeline (see Ross 2003 on these issues). Illicit gemstones and drugs are arguably more crucial to financing rogue conflict entrepreneurs in a greed-based conflict; their omission is a serious flaw. Collier and Hoeffler (2004) do not differentiate different types of natural resources, such as between lootable and non-lootable natural resources (Lujala, Gleditsch & Gilmore 2005), and between point-sourced and diffuse natural resources. Lootable point source natural resources are in particular prone to be illegally exploited and traded. Collier and Hoeffler (2004) are concerned only with past production, neglecting future prospects for extraction (Humphreys 2005). They also focus only on exports, even though production might be a better measure of the availability of these resources, including commodities that were first imported and then re-exported (Humphreys 2005).

A summary of different proxies to measure resource wealth used in cross-country empirical conflict literature follows.

- *Primary commodity* exports as percentage of GDP (Collier & Hoeffler, 2004). This is the indicator from which the initial greed hypothesis is derived, and subsequently became contentious.
- *Agricultural* value added as a percentage of GDP (Humphreys 2005).
- *Oil dependence*; different ways of measuring this have been employed.
  - Oil *production* and *reserves* per capita (Humphreys 2005). This is to distinguish between past and future exploitation of natural resources. Furthermore, Lujala, Rød and Thieme (2007) differentiate oil/hydrocarbon production and reserves into offshore and onshore types. It is the onshore variety that adds to the risk of conflict onset, because offshore facilities can be more easily protected.
  - *Oil rents* per capita, which are further distinguished between *offshore* and *onshore* oil (Ross 2006).
  - *Oil exporter dummy*, when oil exceeds one-third of total exports (Fearon & Laitin 2003).
  - *Oil exports* as a percentage of total exports; Fearon (2005) adds this measure to the Collier–Hoeffler model to specifically locate the oil effect, finding that the effect of primary commodities on conflict is confined to oil.
- *Diamonds*; different ways of measuring diamond wealth have been employed.
  - *Diamond production* per capita (Humphreys 2005). Ross (2006) further disaggregates it into *primary* and *secondary* production to differentiate the unlootable and lootable nature of this resource.
  - *A dummy* for the presence of diamonds, disaggregated further into *primary* and *secondary* types (Lujala, Gleditsch & Gilmore 2005). They find that lootable secondary diamonds increase the risk of civil war onset and its duration, while the primary variety does not. They create mainly ethnic civil wars rather than other forms of civil wars. This risk has been greater since the end of the Cold War. Non-lootable deep mineshaft (primary) diamonds, however, lower

the risk of civil war onset. Lujala (2009) finds a significant positive relationship between gemstone mining and conflict fatalities using spatial information along geographical grids.

- *Resource rents* as a percentage of gross national income (de Soysa & Neumayer 2007). They differentiate between *energy* rents and *mineral* rents; the former consist of oil, gas and coal, while the latter include bauxite, copper, iron ore, lead, nickel, phosphate rock, tin, zinc, gold and silver.
- *Contraband* dummy; conflicts in which a rebel group derives major funds from contraband such as opium, diamonds or coca tend to have longer civil war duration (Fearon 2004). These measures represent both resource dependence and resource abundance, however, and are referred to interchangeably by most studies. This confusion was criticized by Brunnschweiler and Bulte (2008), as indicated in earlier chapters.

Another related issue is the proper specification of the conflict dependent variable in econometric analyses; it can either be the onset or duration of civil war. With regard to onset, the question is whether natural resource wealth increases or decreases the risk or likelihood of civil war; with duration, whether or not it prolongs civil war. Collier and Hoeffler (2004) claim that resource dependence measured by primary goods exports to GDP in increasing the likelihood of civil war onset is significant and robust, while others say that it is not significant (Fearon & Laitin 2003; Fearon 2005; Montalvo & Reynal-Querol 2005; Brunnschweiler & Bulte 2009) or it is not robust (Ross 2004b).[4] On duration, the results are again contradictory. Collier, Hoeffler and Söderbom (2004) find that primary commodities have no significant effect on the duration; but decreases in primary commodity prices would shorten a conflict, since they squeeze rebel finances, when the level of dependence on primary commodity exports is high. Using contraband dummy measures, Fearon (2004) and Ross (2006) find that natural resources lengthen civil war duration; while, using diamond production per capita, Humphreys (2005) finds that this reduces war duration.

---

4. A robust econometric result withstands changes in data coverage concerning, say, the number of conflicts, countries, period of analysis, and so on.

When civil war onset is a dummy (0, 1) variable, an additional complication is the appropriate fatality threshold for coding a case as a civil war/ conflict. There are three variants employed: (a) 1,000 battle-related deaths annually (Collier & Hoeffler 2004); (b) 1,000 battle-related deaths during the course of the conflict (Fearon & Laitin 2003; Fearon 2005); and (c) 25 battle-related deaths annually (de Soysa 2002).

Any measure of natural resource dependence may also be endogenous to conflict, which has two implications: (a) reverse causality, in which civil wars might cause resource dependence by reducing the size of a country's non-resource sector (e.g. manufacturing); and (b) spurious correlation, when both civil war and resource dependence might be independently caused by an unmeasured third variable, such as poor property rights or the weak rule of law.

On reverse causality, Brunnschweiler and Bulte (2009) treat resource dependence, together with per capita income, as endogenous independent variables in their conflict regression, while previous studies always assumed resource dependence to be truly exogenous. They use a set of instruments for resource dependence, as well as income, which consist of a measure of resource abundance, trade openness, the constitution (presidential versus parliamentary systems), absolute latitude, percentage of land in the tropics and distance from the nearest coast or navigable river. They find that, by treating these two variables as endogenous, resource dependence loses its significance and resource abundance has a negative indirect effect on conflict through income. Based on these findings, they reject the previous arguments for placing natural resource wealth or dependence as the principal culprit for civil war. They go on to speculate that resource dependence (a reliance on primary goods exports) may be a manifestation of the failure to grow and diversify as a consequence of conflict, but does not contribute directly to conflict.

On the mechanisms in between conflict and resource dependence, Humphreys (2005), for example, argues that other factors may be present. First, there is the greedy outsider mechanism: the existence of natural resources may be an incentive for third parties – states and corporations – to engage in or indeed foster civil conflict. Second, we have the grievance mechanism: natural resource dependence could in fact be associated with grievances rather than greed. There are at least four variants of this mechanism: (a) countries with middling levels of dependence on natural resources may experience transitory inequality as part of their development process; (b) economies that are dependent on natural resources may be more vulnerable to terms of trade shocks; (c) the process of extraction may produce grievances, as for example, through forced migration; and (d) natural resources wealth may be seen as more unjustly distributed compared to other forms of wealth. Third, there is the weak state mechanism, as also emphasized by Fearon and Laitin (2003). Natural resource dependent economies may be weaker states, a feature that stems from the nature of state revenue, which is mainly dependent on resource rents. On the one hand, untaxed citizens have less ability or incentive to monitor state activity. On the other hand, governments relying more on natural resource rents than on taxation have weak incentives to create strong and accountable bureaucratic structures, similar to the logic of no accountability without taxation, as in Ross (2004a).

On estimation techniques, Fearon (2005) provides the strongest challenge to Collier and Hoeffler's (2004) empirical findings about primary commodity exports and civil war. Fearon, who re-estimates Collier and Hoeffler's model using country/year observations, as opposed to the country/five-year averages employed by Collier and Hoeffler, finds that the significance of statistical associations between primary commodity export and civil war onset vanishes in the country/year regression, meaning that the previous claim of such a relationship existing is simply not robust. In other words, this cross-country result will not withstand variation in sample and data coverage. Most recently, in their cross-country conflict regression, Brunnschweiler and Bulte (2009) also find that the primary commodity export loses its significance when treated as an endogenous variable. A similar view is shared by Ross (2004b), who reviews 14 cross-country empirical studies on natural resource and civil war, complemented with many qualitative study reports. Those studies vary in terms of time coverage, estimation procedures, resource measure, dependent variable construction (different conflict databases and thresholds) and sets of independent variables used; they therefore yield varying results. Ross (2004b) concludes that the claim that primary commodities are associated with the onset of civil war does not appear to be robust, oil dependence appears to be linked to the initiation of conflict, but not its duration, and illicit gemstones and drugs seem to lengthen pre-existing wars. Furthermore, Fearon (2005) shows that the effect of primary commodity exports is confined to oil; this is by adding the variable (oil exports to total exports) into the country/year regression. Humphreys (2005) checks the effect of past oil exploitation (oil production per capita) on civil war onset and finds it positively significant. He asserts that such a relationship works through the weak state mechanism, however; this is by adding interaction terms between measures of natural resource wealth and state strength, measured by (a) a political instability dummy (whether a state has undergone a large change in its political institutions over the past three years; such changes may indicate weakness of state structures); (b) an anocracy dummy (a combination of Fearon and Laitin's instability measure and their "anocracy" measure: it takes the value of 1 if a state is a robust democracy or a robust dictatorship and a 0 otherwise); and (c) the "Weberianness" of state structures, also a measure of state strength. In a similar vein to Humphreys, Fearon (2005) interprets the oil effect as a weak state mechanism rather than a greedy rebel hypothesis; this is by using the correlation between oil export and state weaknesses, measured by government contract observance.

De Soysa and Neumayer (2007) use resource rents data as a percentage of national income (differentiated into energy and mineral rents), and re-estimate both Collier and Hoeffler's (2004a) and Fearon and Laitin's (2003) models using different thresholds for civil war. They find that only energy rents matter for civil war onset, and reject the curvilinear relationship between resource dependence and civil war as proposed by Collier and Hoeffler. De Soysa and Neumayer argue that the significant role of energy rents is more relevant with the weak state mechanism than the greedy rebel hypothesis. I have noted above that several studies also show that only onshore oil and secondary diamonds contribute to civil war onset. A related, and yet unexplored, issue could relate to the ownership of natural resource rents, and what revenue-sharing mechanisms are present between the state and multinational extractive industries, as some arrangements may encourage kleptocracy more.

Facing these challenges, Collier, Hoeffler and Rohner (2009)[5] differentiate between two theories of civil war: "feasibility" and "motivation", which in turn has two variants, i.e. either "greed" or "grievance". But the

---

5. In 2005 an entire issue of the *Journal of Conflict Resolution*, called "Paradigm in Distress", 49 (4), was devoted to demonstrating the non-robustness of the main conclusions of Collier and Hoeffler's greed hypothesis.

content of their previous "greed" hypothesis (now part of motivation) is almost identical with what they now rephrase as "feasibility". If feasibility is about opportunity, greed is also about opportunity. The basic arguments and empirical evidence are much the same as before.

A number of recent studies on the general relationship between commodity booms and the risk of civil war in a cross-country setting are inconclusive. Brückner and Ciccone (2010) find that a drop in commodity prices in resource-dependent sub-Saharan Africa raises the probability of conflict onset. They argue that a fall in growth rates is the channel enhancing conflict risk. They instrument for the reverse causality between growth and conflict by using OECD growth. By contrast, Cotet and Tsui (2013) find that for a historical panel of oil discoveries, after controlling for country fixed effects, the value of oil reserves and civil war are no longer significantly associated. Thus, the contestability of state power and rent-seeking explanations for conflict in the presence of resource rents argument is refuted in this particular study. Bazzi and Blattman (2014) study how commodity price shocks affect civil war onset, duration and intensity. Using different commodity classifications and different definitions of conflict, they find that commodity price booms do not make violent contests for the control of the state more likely. Commodity booms may increase state capacity and may result in the earlier cessation of conflict. By contrast, Lei and Michaels (2014) find that giant oil discoveries increase the risk of conflict, particularly when there is a recent history of conflict. Dube and Vargas (2013) find that, in Colombia, increases in the price of labour-intensive coffee dampen political violence, but rises in the price of capital-intensive oil encourage greater violence, which is in line with the theoretical propositions of Dal Bó and Dal Bó (2011).

In short, the cross-country evidence on resource-curse-led internal conflict is mixed and taxonomic, and depends greatly on variable definition, the time period covered and the number of countries included; by contrast, subnational studies may be more informative.

The first type of subnational studies refers to global cross-sectional analyses where, however, the unit of analysis is a geographical grid, which in most cases is a smaller area and unit of analysis than a nation state. Geographical grids may or may not be resource-rich. For example, not every geographical grid within a resource-rich country is actually resource-rich. But the challenge of finding data on other control variables within a geographical grid may indeed be very difficult.

Cederman, Gleditsch and Buhaug (2013: chap. 5) utilize the G-Econ data set (which is a local-level income data set on geographical grids for 1990), along with a geographically coded political inclusion/exclusion version of their ethnic power relations (EPR) data set. All the data pertains to geographical grids, instead of nations in their cross-sectional analysis. Using a gap (ratio) measure of income horizontal inequality, and political discrimination variables of inclusion, exclusion and recent displacement, they find that income horizontal inequality, political exclusion and the effect of recent political exclusion all significantly affect conflict onset risk in a global cross-section of regions. The coefficients of the political variables are larger, and the interaction between political exclusion and economic horizontal inequality is significant, suggesting that political exclusion and economic disadvantage move together. There are potential issues of reverse causality between conflict and both political and economic disadvantage, which need further analysis, although they are partially addressed by including previous conflict as a control variable. A weakness of the analysis relates to the data limitation on economic horizontal inequalities, as it relates only to 1990. Additionally, economic horizontal inequalities are related to government expenditure; this point is accepted by the authors, but the problem needs more careful handling by looking at local public expenditure.

Buhaug and Rød (2006) use similar geographic grids, and find that proximity to one resource, the more capturable secondary diamonds, enhances conflict risk in Africa. Berman *et al.* (2017), again using geographical grids, demonstrate that sustained positive spikes in commodity prices fuel conflict in various forms in sub-Saharan Africa. Voors *et al.* (2017) analyse the role of subnational data on governance (measured by the potential abuse of power by chieftancies) and secondary diamond location in explaining the intensity and onset of conflict in Sierra Leone, finding no significant effect for either variable.

Indonesia is plagued by several conflicts, some of which are secessionist in nature, while others are inter-communal. Four natural-resource-rich provinces, Aceh, Riau, East Kalimantan and Papua, have wanted to separate, in different degrees, from the federation. Brown (2005) argues that the socio-economic achievements (in terms of jobs and education) of the native Acehnese declined during periods when GRDP (gross regional domestic product, or regional income) rose substantially. This rise in GRDP took place because of the presence of oil and gas in Aceh. For example, poverty in Aceh rose by 239 per cent from 1980 to 2002, whereas it fell by 42 per cent in the rest of Indonesia. In Aceh, income (GRDP) per capita was 39 per cent greater than the Indonesian average but expenditure per head, after redistribution through the fiscal system, was 18 per cent below the national average. In Papua (rich in copper and silver), income per capita was 65 per cent above the national average before the fiscal system came into operation. After taxes and subsidies, expenditure was 9 per cent below the Indonesian average, and there was a higher incidence of poverty, particularly among indigenous peoples. Thus, these separatist tendencies, in whole or in part, are a reflection of the dissatisfaction in some of the richer and natural-resource-endowed areas with the federal authority's redistributive policies of taxing richer provinces to subsidize poorer regions.

Lind, Moene and Willumsen (2014) explore the link between poppy production and conflict in Afghanistan. It is accepted that drug money prolongs conflict, and this is true in this case as well, but the study demonstrates that, when Western casualties are used as a proxy for conflict intensity, there is a positive and significant impact of conflict on opium production using district-level data for 2001 to 2007. There is also little doubt that conflict weakens institutions, and encourages more drug production. The direction of causality is firmly established to be from conflict to opium production, rather than the other way around.

Horizontal inequality as a cause of conflict can work in two directions: the rich may initiate conflict, to extricate themselves from the relatively poor (the rage of the rich); or the poor may rise up, in revolt against the rich (the rage of the poor). The former may be more likely when a region suddenly discovers it can exist viably on its own resources, thus wishing to secede and not hand over revenues to the rest of the country. The latter is more likely to manifest itself in rebellions and revolutionary attempts to overthrow an oppressive state.

In reality, the competing greed versus grievance hypotheses may, after all, be complementary explanations for conflict; this is what is modelled in Appendix 2. In so far as they do provide alternative views, a fair test for their relative explanatory powers is best conducted at the level of a quantitative country case study, because cross-country comparisons of horizontal inequality are still at very early stages of development due to the lack of data. Indonesia's resource-rich regions that have had separatist conflicts with the federal government offer us a striking contrast in trying to gauge the relative explanatory power of the greed versus grievance explanations for conflict. When viewed via the lens of a detailed quantitative case study, the grievance and horizontal inequality explanations dominate any greed motivation. Yet, when looked at as one observation among many through the prism of a cross-country study, Indonesia's resource-rich regions become part of a modified form of the greed explanation (resources helping to prolong the duration of conflict and encouraging secession). It would appear, therefore, that the greed explanation for conflict duration and secessionist wars works in cross-country studies, but has to make way for grievance-based arguments in quantitative country case studies. Grievances and horizontal inequalities may, after all, be better at explaining why conflicts begin, but not necessarily why they persist due to the presence of capturable resource rents. The presence of neither greed nor grievance is sufficient for the outbreak of violent conflict, which requires institutional breakdown; this can be described as the failure of the social contract, and is discussed in Murshed (2010: chap. 5).

Finally, the existing econometric literature regarding the causes of conflict allows us to infer little about the true nature of the causal links between the phenomena examined, particularly when it comes to cross-country empirical evidence. True tests for causality require sufficiently long time series data; unless techniques of time series econometrics are employed, inferences about causality will remain limited in nature.

6

Managing resource rents

Managing resource rents efficiently and equitably is a challenging task, particularly when they are of the mineral, fuel or point-sourced variety. This is mainly because of their non-renewable characteristic, but also because once we regard natural capital as an asset its sustainable depletion involves saving, and investment in other assets – a matter that is addressed by the concept of genuine savings. Furthermore, there are inter-generational equity issues to consider. If a non-renewable asset is to be depleted, arguably some provision needs to be made so that future generations are not entirely deprived of the rents thereof. This chapter addresses some of these issues. I begin by briefly outlining matters related to assigning exploration and extraction rights for minerals and fuels; the next section outlines theoretical issues in connection with genuine saving and sustainability when natural resources are present and utilized for production; I then examine how resource rent windfalls and discoveries should be optimally utilized in the context of consumption, saving, paying off external debt and investment decisions, and whether investments should be in the domestic economy or in international markets. Optimal decision-making in this context can sometimes imply being less concerned about the welfare of future generations compared to the present generation in capital-scarce low-income countries. Finally, the last section considers management issues connected with sovereign or national wealth funds that arise out of saved resource rents. Much of the discussion in this chapter refers to optimal rules and policies in the absence of the mismanagement and policy errors that engender the resource curse.

Assigning exploration rights

On the surface, taxing oil and gas revenues seems not to alter producer behaviour, as these revenues are presumed to remain on stream irrespective of the rate at which they are taxed. But, as Boadway and Keen (2008) point out, the fear that the sovereign owner of these revenues might impose punitive taxes on these flows may actually discourage investment in the development and extraction of these resources; potential investors would therefore need to be assured that future tax burdens will not be excessive. Optimality in non-renewable resource extraction requires that both present and the discounted value of future benefits and costs are internalized in decision-making. Tax revenues from resources can be substantial, but there are considerable uncertainties about the future prices of these commodities, and hence the rent or profit from resource revenues. Designing tax rules is also made difficult by their international nature, because of the fact that there are many tax jurisdictions that have to be taken into account.

In assigning the right to explore, extract or transport oil and gas rents, there may be asymmetrical bargaining power between weak states that are in conflict or have just emerged from conflict, on the one hand, and large multinational extractive firms, on the other. Additionally, there may be asymmetrical information; the host-country government may not know enough about the presence and extent of mineral wealth compared to companies that prospect for them. For these reasons, instead of assigning rights by open negotiation, it might be superior to auction the rights to exploration, extraction and transportation (pipelines) for oil and gas wealth. This is because auctions force companies to reveal information, which they may not do in simple negotiations or tendering (also known as beauty contests).

A succinct summary of issues related to auctioning rights to oil and gas for developing countries is to be found in Cramton (2007). He argues that often there are several issues to be auctioned in relation to exploration, extraction and pipelines, which can be described as "blocks". Sometimes different companies bidding for these may share a common valuation of their profitability, and on occasion the values may be additive (or separable) in their profit reckoning. He also discusses the advantages of sealed- over open-bid auctions. The former reveal more information about bidders, and the latter have a greater ability to prevent collusion among bidders. Cramton (2007) favours simultaneous ascending price auctions or English auctions in general, when bidders have additive values and the competition between them is weak. When competition is stronger, a simultaneous clock auction may be desirable; bidders react with quantities at prices set by the auctioneer. Of course, all the analysis above presumes actions in an ideal situation, when auctioneers or their political masters cannot be corrupted by bidders.

A discussion of the optimal taxation of exhaustible resource rents can be found in Mintz and Chen (2012). Ultimately, states (and their citizens) are the owners of these resources, but oil or mining companies exploit the resources on their behalf. The former can be deemed the principal, and the latter can be considered to be the agent. All arrangements need to be incentive-compatible with the interests of firms. The best form of profit taxation is royalty arrangements on resource rents such that the profit-maximizing interests (rents) of both parties are maximized under competitive conditions. Firms should be able to deduct costs from rents. Furthermore, uniform corporate taxes (on economic income) should be applied nationwide, including on the extractive industry.

Genuine savings and sustainability

Economic agents derive utility mainly from consumption. This utility can also incorporate a host of psychological factors, such as the enjoyment of biodiversity, as well as other behavioural parameters, such as identity-based actions. The flow of goods and services that consumers and citizens enjoy is based on or produced by the stock of capital that the nation owns or borrows. One of the earliest distinctions between the stock of capital or wealth and the flow of income was made by Irving Fisher (1906). The stock of capital is of value only because of the services it produces. The most conventional measure of the flow of national income is gross domestic product, which after adjusting for capital depreciation is known as net domestic product. It is far less common to have systems of accounts for the stock of national capital.

Traditionally, capital referred to only physical capital (machines, inventories, buildings and infrastructure). But an educated and skilled workforce also contributes to a nation's stock of human capital. Environmental economists have now succeeded in including natural capital: the stock of exhaustible resources, land, ecosystems, forests and water resources. Together, all three make up the nation's stock of total capital. Sustainability implies that these stocks of capital, when depleted, need to be replenished such that future generations benefit from an intact stock of wealth. Sustainable growth, therefore, means that the stock of total capital should not be compromised and diminished.

Following Hanley, Dupuy and McLaughlin (2015) (HDM), we can employ this concept to develop the notion of genuine savings, or adjusted net savings, which has been referred to earlier. Genuine savings can be capability- or production-based, when changes in the value of the total stock of wealth must at least be non-negative. Alternatively, it can be outcome- or consumption-based, if real consumption per capita or utility is maintained over time. As HDM (2015) point out, strong sustainability means non-declining natural capital over time, whereas weak sustainability implies that one form of capital can be substituted by another type of capital as long as total wealth is not declining over time. Furthermore, each generation should bequeath an undiminished stock of total capital to the next; see Solow (1974) and Rawls (1971) on this. At any time tastes, technology and the total stock of capital combine to produce national income, via a process known as the resource allocation mechanism (RAM).

Following HDM (2015), let us postulate the following production function for output (Y) in the economy:

$$Y(t) = A(t)F\left[K(t), L(t), R(t)\right] \qquad (6.1)$$

where t refers to a time period, A is a measure of productivity, K is physical capital, L is human capital and R is natural capital. The latter three variables are the inputs into the production process, and all three factors of production are individually necessary for production to take place in the economy.

The following constraint must hold to maintain sustainability:

$$A(t)F\left[K(t), L(t), R(t)\right] \leqq C(t) + \frac{dL(t)}{dt} + \mu L(t) + \frac{dK(t)}{dt} + \lambda K(t)$$

$$(6.2)$$

where C refers to consumption and λ and μ are depreciation rates for physical and human capital respectively. The left-hand side of Equation (6.2) refers to output or aggregate supply; empirically speaking, this is the counterpart of gross domestic or national product in a closed economy. The right-hand side is made up of the uses of output or expenditure. This includes consumption, the augmentation of human (L) and physical capital (K) stocks via investment over time ($d(.)/dt$) and the replacement of depreciation in human and physical capital stocks.

As in Appendix 1, when a representative agent maximizes inter-generational well-being into the future (V) at time t, this depends on successive "instantaneous" utilities (U) as a function of consumption. The utility function has the standard concavity properties, leading to diminishing marginal utility:

$$\text{Max } V(S,t) = \int_{t}^{\infty} [U(C(S,\tau)) e^{-\beta(\tau - t)}] \, dt \qquad (6.3)$$

Here β is the discount rate, τ is the instantaneous utility in a future period and S is the state of the economy associated with stocks of the three sources of wealth (K, L, R). Utility maximization subject to the budget constraint will lead to shadow prices for the three factors of production or sources of wealth.[1] This process incorporates a RAM, including the institutional super-structure of the economy, as it evolves over time. Inter-generational well-being, $V(S(t), t)$, may be time-dependent, and the passage of time could be an investment that augments this stock. Totally differentiating V, we obtain

$$\frac{dV(S(t))}{dt} = \frac{\partial V}{\partial t} + p(t)\frac{dK(t)}{dt} + q(t)\frac{dL(t)}{dt} + n(t)\frac{dR(t)}{dt} \qquad (6.4)$$

The first term on the right-hand side of Equation (6.4) is the increase in well-being over time. The shadow prices of physical, human and natural capital are denoted by p, q and n respectively. These are multiplied by the changes in their stocks over time in the second, third and fourth terms on the right-hand side of (6.4). The interpretation of Equation (6.4) is that the evolution

---

1. Formally, this is the partial derivative of the inter-generational utility (V) with respect to the factor of production or wealth (K, L, R).

of utility over time amounts to the augmentation of all three forms of wealth over time plus an additional factor that raises well-being over time, due to, say, technical progress or increased knowledge. All the three forms of wealth or capital are utilized for production, from which consumption takes place and utility is derived. Weak sustainability requires that the total stock of wealth is undiminished from generation to generation (corresponding to an instantaneous consumption or utility generation point) to maintain constant consumption between and within generations. The equity criterion surrounding sustainability is based on Solow (1974) and the philosopher John Rawls' maximin principle (whereby the greatest benefit is conferred upon the least advantaged members of society).

This leads us to the famous Hartwick (1977) rule, which develops a nexus between consumption and wealth to maintain a sustainable economy. The sufficient condition for constant consumption over time is that all rents from the depletion of non-renewable natural wealth be reinvested into physical or man-made capital. Thus, profits from the depletion of non-renewable resources must be saved. In an imperfect institutional environment, in which rent-seeking and corruption are prevalent, not only will resource depletion exceed the optimal amounts dictated by their competitive shadow prices, but resource rents could also be squandered (not saved) from a national perspective.

Technical progress which raises the productivity of physical capital implies that earlier generations can have a higher consumption to capital ratio provided that they can bequeath a sufficient quantity of technical-progress-adjusted capital to future generations. Population growth augments the stock of human capital, but may cause congestion and environmental degradation, which reduces the stock of per capita natural capital. Sustainability requires the addition of extra stocks of time-dependent capital.

Complications can arise in an open economy that is not perfectly integrated in the Heckscher–Ohlin–Samuelson sense, whereby factor prices and product prices are internationally equalized with no regulatory impediments to trade. In an open economy, nations can maintain the rules of sustainability domestically but collude with their violation abroad by importing unsustainably extracted non-renewable, or even renewable, natural-resource-based products. One can imagine that was so in the earlier industrial ages associated with colonialism. Chichilnisky (1994) shows that in an open economy ill-defined property rights can increase resource depletion above optimal levels in an institutionally weak nation. National governments may promote inter-generational equity, but no international organization does so in an open economy context. Resource rent windfalls caused by booms in commodity prices can lead to the relaxation of the Hartwick rule above, but in practice they do not appear to be substantial (HDM 2015).

Empirically speaking, ever since the mid-1990s the World Bank has been publishing data related to genuine savings, which is annually updated. Here non-renewable natural capital (fuels, metals and minerals) is valued at the world price net of extraction or production cost. Renewable natural capital usage that exceeds its natural growth is deducted from genuine savings. Education expenditure, which augments human capital, is added to saving. Pollution damage is deducted from savings. HDM (2015) point to historical data on genuine savings for mature economies such as the United States, United Kingdom and Germany. In the United States genuine savings were positive except during the two world wars and the Great Depression in the twentieth century. In the United Kingdom genuine savings were negative during the early Industrial Revolution and the two world wars. In Germany they were negative only during the Second World War and its aftermath. Thus, avoiding the resource curse implies non-negative genuine savings except for the poorest capital-scarce developing countries. In econometric models, genuine savings data are a poor predictor of future consumption when the time period considered is relatively short (HDM 2015).

Another rule in connection with the optimal extraction of non-renewable resources is the Hotelling (1931) rule, which states that the extraction path should be along lines such that the net price of the resource (price minus extraction costs) increases at a rate equal to the rate of time preference or the interest rate. Resource prices are not observed to increase at this rate, however, but, rather, are found to be subject to considerable volatility.

Consumption and investment decisions emanating from resource rent windfalls

The discussion above was concerned with optimal and sustainable rules for wealth management in the context of an *existing* endowment of natural capital. What occurs when new sources of natural wealth are discovered, typically non-renewable minerals and fuels, which augment the capital stock? The income and rents thus generated may be regarded as a *windfall*. The permanent income hypothesis (PIH) would suggest an increase in consumption or domestic absorption, and the constant consumption (Ramsey) rule implies consumption smoothing. This entails saving in a sovereign wealth fund (SWF) that is high enough to yield interest income or profits so as to maintain the increased level of consumption constant into the future (in theory, for all time). If we denote ΔR as the increase in the resource endowment and r as the rate of interest, with PV_t being the present value at time t, then the change in consumption (ΔC) following the analysis in Venables and Wills (2016) is

$$\Delta C = r\Delta R = rRPV_t \qquad (6.5)$$

In other words, there is a permanent increase in consumption whose increase is equal to the annuity value of the new resource value. The property of constant consumption is retained as in the previous section.

As pointed out by Venables (2016), other analysts, such as Barnett and Ossowski (2003) of the IMF, suggest an even more conservative "bird-in-hand" approach in which all revenues are gradually built up as savings in an SWF, and the increase in consumption confined to only the interest earned by the SWF.[2]

Either of these two policy rules can be applied to capital-abundant high-income economies, such as Norway, or many of the states in the Arabian Gulf, such as Kuwait and Qatar. But, as van der Ploeg and Venables (2011), as well as Venables and Wills (2016) and Wills, Senbet and Simbanegavi (2016), point out, the situation is different in capital-scarce and poor low-income economies. Capital scarcity implies a high interest rate well above world interest rates; greater poverty means less concern should be present about relatively richer future generations; moreover, the economy may be saddled with external debt. In this situation it is optimal to increase domestic consumption, liquidate some external debt and engage in domestic private

---

2. Note that the interest earned on the SWF is cumulative over time; in the beginning only a small amount of the rents is available in the SWF; gradually this fund accumulates over time.

and public investment.[3] Being capital-scarce implies that the marginal prod-uctivity of capital is greater there than in mature economies. Therefore, these countries are on a potentially higher growth trajectory; the resource rent windfall can help bring forward the increase in domestic absorption. Saving in an SWF invested in international capital markets is not an optimal policy (van der Ploeg & Venables 2011; Wills, Senbet & Simbanegavi 2016; Venables & Wills 2016) except in the case of very large resource rent windfalls and other considerations, elaborated on below.

In order to illustrate the differences between developed and capital-scarce countries it is instructive to examine the optimal equation for the growth of consumption, c. Following Venables and Wills (2016),

$$c = \sigma(r - \beta) \tag{6.6}$$

where $\sigma = CU''(C)/U'(C)$, the elasticity of the marginal utility of consump-tion, capturing the fact that future generations may be richer than the present generation in poorer countries, and have a lower utility from con-sumption at the margin. Recall that β is the discount rate, and in advanced economies characterized by "perfect" capital markets the interest rate is equal to the discount rate and time preference, such that the *growth* in con-sumption in Equation (6.6) is zero. The PIH implies a one-shot increase in consumption.

In capital-scarce developing countries this is not the case, not least because the interest rate is greater than the world interest rate, because of capital scarcity and imperfect access to world capital markets (for borrowing purposes). Venables and Wills (2016), as well as van der Ploeg and Venables (2011), postulate that the so-called interest rate premium on domestic interest rates in "developing" countries is an increasing function of external debt (D), such that in those economies $r'(D) > 0$ and $r(D) > r$ or r^*, the "world" interest rate. We would need to rewrite Equation (6.6) as

$$c = \sigma(r(D) - \beta) \tag{6.7}$$

---

3. Bhattacharyya and Collier (2014) empirically demonstrate that, for a panel of countries, increases in resource rents over the period from 1970 to 2005 led to a decline in public investment. This policy error is yet another symptom of the resource curse.

This means that the growth in consumption is positive, and the availability of new resource rents (ΔR) relaxes the economy's budget constraint. If the economy has pre-existing debt its budget constraint needs to be rewritten as

$$K(t) + L(t) + R(t) - D(t) \qquad (6.8)$$

During the existence of the resource rent stream it is optimal to reduce some external debt, but asset accumulation is less than what would be postulated by the permanent income hypothesis for a richer economy. With a larger resource windfall it may be optimal to pay off all external debt, and with very large streams of resource rents an SWF may be optimal.

The paper by van der Ploeg and Venables (2011) analyses several resource boom scenarios in low-income, capital-scarce developing countries. A small and temporary resource rent windfall optimally leads to a jump in consumption, and the rate of growth of consumption declines as the resource rents peter out. If the resource is anticipated in advance then there is an advance jump in consumption proportionate to the windfall, which is greater the larger the windfall, and the earlier rents are expected to come on stream.

There is also scope for investment in domestic capital, particularly public capital, to avoid the policy-induced resource curse distortion of under-investment in infrastructure and public capital, indicated by Bhattacharyya and Collier (2014). Investment in infrastructure may be output-enhancing, particularly when complementary to private investment. In addition, high-social- but low-financial-return projects with long time horizons can be a focus for domestic investment out of resource rents (Wills, Senbet & Simbanegavi 2016). In a nutshell, developing countries should engage in both domestic public and private investment in capital and infrastructure, as well as reduce their international debt.

Arezki and Sy (2016) argue that, as far as investment in domestic infrastructure is concerned, development banks should initiate these investments, as they are more informed about high-social-return but high-cost projects and also have greater skills in managing risky projects. Commercial banks are loath to lend to long-term projects after the Basel III accords, which require their asset portfolio longevities to be commensurate with their short-term liabilities. Once the projects have reached fruition and are financially viable they may be taken over by arm's-length investors in the private sector, according to Arezki and Sy (2016), as well as Amoako-Tuffour (2016), with an open question as to whether national SWFs should participate in these or not. Arezki and Sy (2016) argue for the development of a bond market in the African context to finance arm's-length investment in infrastructure.

In summary, for poorer countries resource rent windfalls should optimally lead to less investment of savings from resource rents into SWFs compared to wealthier resource-rich economies such as Norway. This is because of their relative poverty and capital scarcity. These poorer countries are also potentially on a greater growth trajectory, so resource rents should allow them to enhance domestic absorption (consumption and investment) earlier. There is a case for retiring some external debt, which may lower interest rates on borrowing from international capital markets.

Investment of some of the savings in world capital markets may be desirable for at least two other reasons, however, leaving aside political economy considerations. The first is to do with the lack of domestic absorptive capacity. If investments in public infrastructure and growth-enhancing public education and health expenditure cannot be made because of supply bottlenecks and macroeconomic problems then there is a case for temporarily "parking" these funds in international financial markets akin to an SWF. Domestic capacity, in terms of human capital (doctors, nurses, teachers, engineers) to operate the public infrastructure, may need to be built up.

Furthermore, there are macroeconomic issues related to the "Dutch disease" analysed in Chapter 3. New resource rents lead to real exchange rate appreciation. This can be brought about by nominal exchange rate appreciation and/or inflation. The former mechanism is restricted in nominal fixed exchange rate regimes, in which inflation is the main mechanism. If the central bank tightens monetary policy on account of inflation, there may be a recession. In that event, looser fiscal policy may help. Furthermore, in the presence of low absorptive capacity in the economy for the new resource rents, it is better for them to be "parked" in a savings fund akin to an SWF to avoid some of the consequences of the Dutch disease involving inflation, real exchange rate appreciation and the crowding out of the traded sector. Both the first two problems are exacerbated when revenues are anticipated in advance of their coming on stream.

Second, there is a case for a stabilization fund to counter volatility in resource revenues as their world prices fluctuate over the commodity price boom–bust cycle, and has been discussed for nearly 70 years, most famously by Prebisch (1950). Additionally, it is well known in the literature on risky behaviour that *prudent* risk-averse economic agents faced with volatile or uncertain expected future incomes may have a precautionary motive for saving.[4]

An early case for such a stabilization fund was made by Hasson (1956). Stabilization funds may be the answer, but such funds must have clear and robust rules of management, as many stabilization funds in the past have gone awry (see Wills, Senbet & Simbanegavi 2016; and Venables & Wills 2016). A good current example of a well-managed and sound stabilization fund is for copper in Chile (see Chapter 4). Compared to SWFs, stabilization funds need to be more liquid, so that the funds can be utilized readily. The main purpose is to smooth government revenues over the boom and bust commodity price cycle. Barnett and Ossowski (2003), among others, argue that there is limited coordination of these stabilization resource funds with the budgetary process, and there is weak overall monitoring of the funds. Sugawara (2014) demonstrates that, for a sample of 68 resource-rich economies over the period from 1988 to 2012, the existence of stabilization funds did smooth government expenditure. But with sound fiscal rules and natural resource management there may be no need for stabilization funds. There is a long history of failed stabilization funds in the past, with a particularly poignant example (Nauru) mentioned in Wills, Senbet and Simbanegavi (2016).

Sovereign wealth fund management and the externalities on governance

Sovereign wealth funds, defined as state-owned international funds, are growing in number and fashion, even in the case of capital-scarce developing countries in Africa. Not all are a consequence of non-renewable resource rents; some may be a means of investing cumulatively huge current account surpluses in the balance of payments, as is the case for China and Singapore. But, as Frynas (2017) indicates, the majority of developing country SWFs

---

4. The third derivative of the utility function with respect to consumption, encompassing anticipated or expected future risky incomes, is positive.

are related to rents from non-renewable extractive sectors. Some of the largest SWFs are owned by capital-surplus oil-, gas- or mineral-dependent economies such as Abu Dhabi, Qatar, Saudi Arabia and Malaysia. Some SWFs are also pension funds. A full discussion of SWFs is beyond the scope of this work; see, for example, the chapters in Cummings *et al.* (2017) as an example of this literature.

As indicated in the previous section, the motives for these differ among countries, and there is a stronger argument for capital-abundant and richer economies investing in this manner in equities in international financial markets. Lower-income, capital-scarce, developing countries are also setting up SWFs, but their developmental objectives are different, including temporary parking rents to avoid Dutch disease, saving some present-day rents for future generations and building up funds for future domestic investment. For richer developing countries, SWFs are a policy riposte to growing globalization and "financialization",[5] colourfully referred to as "vulture developmentalism"; see Haberly (2017), for example. The development of financialization has been associated with a growing number of episodes of financial and currency crises in developing countries. SWFs, in addition to the holding of the more liquid foreign exchange reserves, are part of the strategic response to these crises by middle-income emerging economies. SWFs can also be a means of obtaining technology transfer from developed countries and fostering industrialization or economic diversification in the face of constraints on traditional infant industry policies emanating from WTO rules, and the stringent enforcement of intellectual property rights under the same agreements. That said, the inter-generational transfer motive and the high return on "financial" assets in recent times are also important motives. For example, it has been estimated that the assets of SWFs grew by 59.1 per cent in just five years between 2008 and 2013, and more than 32 new SWFs were created.[6]

For poorer and relatively capital-scarce economies, SWFs or international savings funds constitute a means of temporarily maximizing the value and growth of rents for future domestic absorption, as demonstrated in the previous section. But there may be political economy considerations as well (Amoako-Tuffour 2016); SWFs are a means of reducing the pilferage

---

5. This is a term utilized to emphasize the focus on share price value, as opposed to other managerial objectives (see, for instance, Haberly 2017).
6. See www.swfinstitute.org/sovereign-wealth-fund (accessed 21 January 2018).

of resource rents and kleptocratic tendencies, although SWFs cannot completely insulate society from these proclivities.

SWFs have a long history, particularly if one includes pension funds. Frynas (2017) indicates that one of the earliest non-OECD country SWFs was created by Kuwait in 1953. Many US states and Canadian provinces operate SWFs. Wills, Senbet and Simbanegavi (2016) discuss the Norwegian case. Following the discovery of North Sea oil in 1969, the fiscal position of the Norwegian state fluctuated with oil prices, leading to the creation of the Norwegian SWF, which is cited as the prime exemplar of the sound management of an oil-based SWF, which has both pension fund maximization and inter-generational transfer as objectives.

Amoako-Tuffour (2016) argues that when SWFs do exist in capital-scarce and low-income developing countries, as in Africa, they should align themselves towards domestic investment in infrastructure, particularly in capital-poor sub-Saharan African economies. Gelb *et al.* (2014) are less sanguine, arguing that infrastructural investment should mostly come out of the normal budgeting process. They point out that in 2012 at least 56 per cent of all SWFs were, however, exposed to financing domestic infrastructure. They point to several factors crucial to sound public investment management. These include sound project appraisal, good project selection, budgeting, monitoring implementation and project evaluation via audits. Amoako-Tuffour (2016) explicitly points to the multiple objectives of the Nigerian and Ghanaian SWFs. These countries have multiple funds matching varying objectives: stabilization, inter-generational transfer and investment in domestic infrastructure. Interestingly, Angola, a major oil producer, operates a single fund.

Gelb *et al.* (2014) discuss in detail management issues related to SWFs that arise from extractable resource rents. They point to the variable record in the management of these SWFs, with considerable off-budget and non-transparent public expenditures from these SWFs. Papua New Guinea and Venezuela provide examples of poorly managed SWFs (Frynas 2017). Furthermore, Gelb *et al.* (2014) argue that many stabilization funds have not yet succeeded in developing genuinely fiscal policies for their states. In their view, linking domestic investment to SWFs can further exacerbate the risks of poor management. These risks may be minimized by ensuring that they do not destabilize the macroeconomy, by investment via partnerships, transparency in operations and ensuring that the management of the SWFs is independent and professional. Moreover, projects with a high social value but with low financial returns should be financed from the budget and not the investment arms of SWFs, as these can jeopardize the long-term financial viability of SWFs. More generally, the presence of multiple objectives within a single body may compromise the ability to meet any of these individually.

Mention should be made of the Santiago Principles, which define good corporate governance practice by SWFs. These incorporate 24 voluntary standards in SWF management, ranging from governance to accountability and transparency issues (Frynas 2017). In addition, as Gelb *et al.* (2014) point out, there has to be a strict separation between ownership and the regulation or supervision of SWFs for them to be managed efficiently. Often this means independent boards that supervise or regulate.

Frynas (2017) draws attention to the Truman ratings of SWFs, which ask "Yes"/"No" questions related to the structure, governance, transparency and accountability of the fund. These indicators may be supplemented by the Resource Governance Index created by the Revenue Watch Institute, which encompasses the quality of governance in 58 extractable resource-rich countries. Frynas (2017) correlates these indicators with some of the World Bank's governance scores (Kaufman, Kraay and Mastruzzi 2006) for regulatory quality and the rule of law. For developed OECD countries, he finds that both types of scores are high. For some countries, such as Oman and Qatar, although the regulatory quality and rule of law scores are high, the governance of natural resources and the Truman index scores are low. Exactly the opposite applies to the ex-Soviet republics of Azerbaijan and Kazakhstan, as well as Timor-Leste and Trinidad and Tobago, which do poorly in general governance scores but their SWF and resource regulation scores are high. Azerbaijan, for example, has a well-managed state oil fund (SOFAZ), but the national budgetary process is regarded to be corrupt and opaque.

Another question relates to whether or not the presence of SWFs contributes towards *enhancing* good governance in extractable-resource-rich countries. It can be argued that nations that are governed by good institutions and that also have sound fiscal and monetary policies do not need SWFs as a means to improving governance and controlling kleptoc-racy. Tsani (2015) finds that SWFs do contribute towards better governance. Her methodology involves quantile regressions, which separate the sample in order of initial relative performance. Her indicators of governance are from the Kaufmann, Kraay and Mastruzzi (2006) World Bank scores on government effectiveness, rule of law and the control of corruption. The period of analysis is from 1996 to 2007. The minimum period taken by a SWF to impact on governance is ten years. Control variables include GDP per capita as a measure of development, trade openness, population density and other cultural indicators (religion, fraction of population speaking English). The data is tested on two samples of countries: a resource-rich sample of 27 countries, and a more general sample of 81 countries.

Her results suggest a significant impact of SWFs on the quality of governance both in countries that initially had high governance scores and in those that were at the lower end of the spectrum in terms of the quality of governance. This suggests that SWFs could be a mechanism for improving governance and avoiding the resource curse.

Lastly, mention should be made of the Extractive Industries Transparency Initiative.[7] This was set up by a number of development non-governmental organizations (NGOs), with the backing of the British government, in 2003 to minimize corruption surrounding rents from extractive industries (Brouder 2009). It is a voluntary initiative that has 52 members, encouraging transparency and the disclosure of payments made by mining and oil/gas companies, as well as the revenues accruing to the state from extractive industries. The initiative is maintained through contributions from individual governments, resulting in the EITI Multi-Donor Trust Fund, run by the World Bank. Papyrakis, Rieger and Gilberthorpe (2017) examine the effects of the EITI on corruption econometrically in a panel of several countries. They also analyse various stages in EITI implementation, finding that EITI membership moderates tendencies towards corruption in extractable-resource-rich countries.

---

7. There are other similar initiatives, such as the Global Mining Initiative and the Kimberley process for certifying diamonds.

7

Concluding comments

The modern resource curse literature can be traced back to the 1970s, when it concerned itself mainly with macroeconomic problems faced by economies that had received a windfall income from a commodity or oil price boom. This literature, known as the "Dutch disease" literature, was not necessarily focused on developing countries. Rather, the emphasis was on the inflationary pressures brought on by greater spending power, and real exchange rate appreciation, including possibilities of nominal exchange rate overshooting. There was also the spectre of unemployment increasing if there was a strong wealth effect on money demand from the resource windfall. There would be a change in the economy's steady-state equilibrium composition of output, away from traded goods to non-traded goods, on account of the real exchange rate appreciation. In practice, it meant some deindustrialization. The analytical models underlying these processes can be found in the literature published mainly in the 1980s, as for example, in Neary and van Wijnbergen (1986) and Murshed (1997: chap. 6).

The commodity (mainly oil) price booms of the 1970s indirectly contributed to the developing country debt crisis in Latin America and elsewhere in the 1980s. Due to the lack of domestic absorptive capacity in many capital-surplus oil-rich economies, some of the oil rents or petro-dollars were invested in international capital markets. This played a part in increased lending by Western commercial banks to other developing countries, culminated in the developing country debt crisis[1] of the 1980s when Mexico defaulted on servicing its debt in 1982 (Ffrench-Davis & Devlin 1995).

---

1. Petro-dollars were not the sole cause of the Latin American debt crisis of the 1980s.

Initially, the Dutch disease literature had developed economies such as the Netherlands, Norway and the United Kingdom in mind. Later there were extensions of Dutch disease to developing countries, including the effects of large-scale guest worker remittances (see, for example, Lartey, Mandelman & Acosta 2012), as well as the effects of foreign aid (for example, Fielding & Gibson 2013): unrequited transfers that worked very much like resource windfalls. The term "resource curse" was popularized following Auty (1993) to describe the economic failures of resource-rich economies. In addition to the macroeconomic problems created by real exchange rate overvaluation, a host of other problems were discovered in many resource-rich countries, including the fact that their growth performance seemed to lag behind resource-poor countries during the 1980s and 1990s. At the turn of the new millennium, and soon afterwards, there appear to have been grave policy errors in many resource-rich developing countries. As expanded on above, these concern macroeconomic policy errors and the inability of economies to undertake structural change, including acquiring manufacturing competitiveness, institutional failure and the descent into civil war in some cases.

What can be done to avoid these dangers? Starting with macroeconomic issues, there need to be counter-cyclical macroeconomic policies across the commodity price boom–bust cycle. This is true of both monetary and fiscal policies. Frankel (2012) suggests the adoption of an initial stance of foreign exchange reserve accumulation during the early stages of a commodity price boom. This can prevent inflation, and excessive real exchange rate appreciation. At a more convenient later juncture, some real exchange rate appreciation can be allowed for.

Frankel (2012) also argues that monetary policy should target export product prices such that the real exchange rate is allowed to appreciate when commodity export prices are high, and the converse should be permitted when commodity prices are low. Monetary policies that are only inflation-oriented risk appreciating the currency when import prices are high, as during a commodity price decline. Frankel (2012) also advocates the denomination of debt, particularly external debt, in commodity prices for resource-dependent economies. So, for example, an oil exporter should fix its external debt in terms of oil prices. Hence, when this particular price dips, debt servicing costs diminish, and vice versa. Such a policy could be established by getting the lending of international financial institutions such as the World Bank and IMF to these countries denominated in commodity prices

The effects of volatility in commodity prices can be mitigated by the hedging of export proceeds in option markets (Frankel 2012). But such a policy does not allow countries to benefit from upswings in commodity prices, although, interestingly, one country – Mexico – utilizes options only for a downswing in oil prices, allowing it to gain from oil price increases. Fiscal policies also need to be counter-cyclical, the best example being that of Chile, which has explicit fiscal rules about the budgetary process, as described in Chapter 4. Malaysia and Botswana, too, have been fiscally prudent, as we have also seen in Chapter 4. The idea is to have fiscal surpluses during commodity price booms, and utilize these later during downswings in the economy or commodity prices. The failure to do so increases the risk of the resource curse, as was the case in nearly all unsuccessful resource-rich economies. Frankel (2012) points out that many developing countries have adopted counter-cyclical fiscal policy stances since 2000. Several resource-rich economies continue to remain heavily dependent on revenues derived from natural resource rents.

This brings us to the role of investing in international capital markets, the sovereign wealth funds discussed in Chapter 6. Sustainability requires that the net value of a nation's total wealth should not be allowed to diminish, but when it discovers new resources other considerations arise. The general rule from the permanent income hypothesis is that countries increase their consumption or absorption by the annuity value of the windfall. In our present financially globalized era, this means investing in an SWF. It also meets the demands of inter-generational equity. But capital-scarce developing countries, which have the conditions for greater growth and in which future generations are likely to be considerably richer than the present generation, should consume and invest some of these windfall gains. They should also choose to retire some of their existing external debt. The failure to do so leads to countries succumbing to the resource curse, as was the case in Nigeria and Bolivia in the past.

There may be other reasons, however, for capital-scarce and low-income developing countries parking their funds in an SWF. One is the absence of sufficient domestic absorptive capacity to absorb the rents, in which case there is likely to be high inflation and generalized kleptocracy. Second, parked funds may be the source of the counter-cyclical fiscal stabilizers discussed above. Finally, and above all, arm's-length SWFs can be justified on political economy grounds. The accumulation of foreign exchange reserves, as well as SWFs, makes it difficult for corrupt individuals to dissipate resource rents, and it moderates the voracity effect discussed in Chapter 3. The SWFs need to be professionally and independently managed, with financial considerations chiefly in mind, and an absence of many conflicting objectives. This is why, perhaps, many developing countries new to these types of investments have chosen to have several funds that are separated in their objectives of inter-generational transfers, infrastructural investment and fiscal revenue stabilization. But it has to be recognized that the increased developing country interest in SWFs is greatly driven by the financialization of the global economy, making these financial investments very attractive not just in terms of their returns but also as an entry point into the global production chain.

Are resource-rich, or resource-dependent, economies less able to bring about structural change in their economies? As has been repeatedly emphasized over decades, structural change is central to modern economic growth. Rapid economic growth is usually associated with industrialization, because of its greater potential for technical progress and productivity growth. This is a point made by economists such as Clark (1940), and more recently by Chenery (1979). Thus, rising per capita incomes are associated with a greater share of secondary activities or manufacturing in the economy. The seminal work of Lewis (1954) was concerned with utilizing surplus labour in an agrarian economy to foster manufacturing output, economic growth and development, leading to the eventual exhaustion of the surplus labour associated with underdevelopment.

Few nations enter the ranks of the international economy as manufacturing exporters; at first they export commodities associated with their natural resource endowment (Chenery 1979), before structural changes in the economy take place. These changes do not take place in an institutional vacuum, and require the presence and functioning of growth-promoting institutions, as elaborated in Acemoglu, Johnson and Robinson (2002, 2005). The important point made by Chenery (1979) is that international specialization in primary commodities is a symptom of "deferred" industrialization, something that Prebisch (1950) and Singer (1950) argue should occur sooner rather than later due to their belief in the secular decline in the relative price of primary goods. Ergo, commodity price booms and resource dependence, at the very least, *delay* the structural transformation of the economy towards manufacturing.

Structural issues associated with the Dutch disease have been analysed in Chapter 2. Here I have pointed out the conditions under which a resource boom does not crowd out the traded sector (East Asian case), and when it is more likely to occur (Latin American case). Judicious policy design can lead to avoidance of the shrinking of the more dynamic traded sector of the economy. This may permit countries to avoid missing the acquisition of manufacturing competitiveness by not allowing excessive real exchange rate overvaluation along with policies to promote competitive industrialization. Therefore, the disease is not inevitable, as the case studies of Malaysia and Chile in Chapter 4 attest to. SWFs also allow for technology transfer, and participation in global value chains in manufacturing.

This optimistic picture regarding the avoidance of the main scourge of the Dutch disease through policy inoculation has to be tempered by the more dystopic features of premature deindustrialization depicted by Rodrik (2016). There is a tendency for the manufacturing share of employment and value added to decline at lower per capita income levels in present-day developing countries compared to this process when it took place among the earlier industrializers in the developed world. Latin American and sub-Saharan economies, in particular, have deindustrialized prematurely, despite experiencing productivity improvements. This is partly a consequence of the external competition induced by globalization making imports of manufactures cheaper, but also to some extent a result of these country's economies being more natural-resource-dependent (Palma 2014). Meanwhile, East Asian countries have sped ahead and increased their global market share of manufacturing goods. The discussion in Chapter 6 suggests that SWFs could be a means of indirectly participating in the activities of high-tech multinational firms, a process curiously described as "vulture developmentalism" (Haberly 2017).

As also indicated in Chapter 2, the resource curse may have been absent, historically, at least in the regions of recent settlement making up present-day North America and Australasia. The application of the "Christopher Columbus" model (Findlay & Lundahl 1994) results in forward and backward linkages from resource-based production to manufacturing. The primary and the manufacturing sectors were both expanded under the stimulus provided by the huge growth in world trade during the first era of globalization from 1870 to 1914, brought about by falling transport costs. There could be the vertical (mining) and horizontal (agriculture) expansion of an endogenous land frontier driven by the twin stimuli of rising commodity prices (greater demand from industrialized countries) and a diminished cost of capital (induced by international financial flows). Real wages increased, despite large-scale immigration accommodating the extension of the land frontier. Furthermore, even when there was a reliance on a staple product, as in Canada, the economy could evolve new staples, after demand for older staples declined (Innis 1930).

In the tropical developing countries of today, the picture was quite different. Findlay and Lundahl (1999) emphasize the heterogeneity between plantation economies, mining economies, peasant economies and mixed economies, analogous to the distinction between point and diffuse resource-dependent economies. In all these economies the first, "golden" age of globalization saw an increase in demand for commodities, the introduction of new commodities for production and the discovery of minerals. The presence of surplus labour or immigrant labour from India, China and Malaya inhibited wage growth, and linkages to manufacturing growth were muted, if at all present, despite the vent for surplus generated by new trading opportunities (Myint 1958). Thus, the stimulus for the development of domestic manufacturing was either weak or absent in most tropical (developing) countries. There were, however, positive advances in infrastructural development.

If the economic resource curse can be labelled "Dutch disease", a political side to this phenomenon also exists. Moreover, the politics and the economics interact, and not necessarily in any particular order; politics and economics are consequently *inseparable*. The literature on the institutional resource cure has burgeoned in the last two decades, and has two strands. One set focuses on institutional quality driving the existence and extent of the resource curse. The other genre in this body of knowledge looks at the impact of resource discoveries, commodity price booms and resource dependence, on political institutions and the quality of governance.[2] I review both aspects of the institutional resource curse in Chapters 3

---

2. Utilizing the language of econometrics, the first strand in this literature employs institutions as an independent variable in, say, a growth regression, and the second strand deploys institutions as the dependent variable. Combining the two would involve a two-stage process, described above.

and 4, including the cross-sectional evidence on the subnational resource curse. Of course, only developing countries are considered to have poor institutions!

Institutions contribute to the resource curse via their impact on growth, and this literature emerged later than the macroeconomic "Dutch disease" literature. Mehlum, Moene and Torvik (2006) describe these as grabber-friendly institutions. Lane and Tornell (1996) describe voracity effects; Hodler (2006) analyses the effect of windfall rents on rent-seeking contests; Murshed (2010: chap. 2) theoretically models growth collapse engendered by rent-seeking contests in a weak institutional setting. Furthermore, there is a literature on how resource rents impact on the incentives of rulers. There is also a smaller literature on how resource rents impact upon other variables of interest in the growth process, such as education (see Chapter 3).

The political resource curse literature per se focuses on how resource rents and windfalls impact on political institutions and governance. Chief among them is the effect that increased resource rents have on strengthening an existing autocracy (Caselli & Tesei 2016), retarding democratic development and accountability (Ross 2001) and encouraging corruption and weaker governance structures.

The approach taken in Mavrotas, Murshed and Torres (2011) and Murshed, Badiuzzaman and Pulok (2015) represents a combination of the two strands in the resource curse literature: first, resource rents impact on governance and democratic quality; later, the institutions determined by the presence or emergence of resource rents govern the process of economic growth. Evidence for the cross-country institutional resource curse may be getting weaker (Metcalfe 2007; Boschini, Petterson & Roine 2013; Murshed, Badiuzzaman & Pulok 2015). Perhaps the pressure exerted by bilateral and multilateral donors has improved governance and democratic quality, or it may be that the established institutional data sets no longer capture the adroit, nuanced and surreptitious autocratic and corrupt practices that have been emerging and evolving in recent years.[3]

Resource rents, particularly those related to extractable sectors, especially oil and diamonds, contribute to enhanced civil war risk. This literature is reviewed in Chapter 5. In explaining civil war, what was primarily

---

3. This is, broadly speaking, argued by the investigators creating the V-Dem data set mentioned in Chapter 4.

believed to represent elite competition over rents gradually evolved into a greater emphasis being placed on resource rents becoming a source of local grievance; this therefore fuelled conflict, taking the form not just of civil war but also of protest and confrontation. In a nutshell, this literature, which is currently growing and developing, emphasizes the distributional conflict engendered by resource rents at the *local* or subnational level. At a more fundamental level, the role of resource rents in causing conflict is related to the chain of causation in the institutional resource curse literature in explaining long-run growth. The conditions for growth retardation and conflict risk enhancement are similar, such as the availability of capturable rents.

The common thread running through the resource curse literature, based on the link between policy failure in addressing the Dutch disease, and its long-term consequences, and the process of institutional malfunctioning (the political resource curse), lies in the *endogeneity* of policies (Acemoglu, Johnson & Robinson 2002, 2005). Economic policies are determined by the political process, which in turn determines the degree of economic progress, after controlling for agency and serendipity. The degree of economic progress or retardation can then, in turn, affect the political process.

As far as institutional reform is concerned, little can be done about inherited institutions, but it may be possible to do something to reduce or minimize the chances of Mother Earth's gifts becoming a source of (greater) corruption among the great and the good. Chapter 6 reviews a paper (Tsani 2015) that presents cross-country evidence in a panel data quantile regression showing that SWFs could be just the commitment technology to promote good governance in resource-rich economies. Tsani's results apply generally to countries starting out with low-quality, as well as those beginning with higher-quality, governance. SWFs may exert a separation of powers or arm's-length influence reducing corruption.

This brings us to the new directions being taken in research on the resource curse. As we have noted, the cross-country empirical evidence on the resource curse, and also the within-country cross-regional empirical analysis, produces mixed and inconclusive results on whether the resource curse exists or not. This has resulted in many suggestions, such as by van der Ploeg and Poelhekke (2017), to focus future research on case studies. These involve the analysis of localized individual cases of the resource curse. No doubt we shall also see the current fashion and obsession with experimental methodologies in economics being increasingly extended to resource curse problems and case studies.

The methodologies of anthropology, and its cognate discipline, political ecology, have always been good in analysing local case studies. Localized studies inform and remind us that a sea of success can conceal droplets of failure; equally a country may have successes without being a success. This literature is vast, and beyond the scope of a book on the economics of the resource curse. A brief mention is in order, however. Gilberthorpe and Rajak (2017: 200) speak of "recontextualising the study of resource extraction in the social relations in which it is embedded". They speak of the development of comparative case studies (multi-site ethnographies), and the study of the moral, cultural and political apparatus employed by extractive multinationals. They refer to a new scramble for the natural resources located in Africa, arguing that technical solutions to a fundamentally political problem are insufficient, and that they require close inspection of social relations. Porter and Watts (2017) describe a Nigerian subnational success story, Edo state. Despite the odds, and in the context of a nation not known for good governance, resource-rich Edo state's achievements have been impressive. They include internally generated revenue, capital expenditure contracts that are completed, an education level higher than the Nigerian average level thanks to the availability of mass free education, and a poverty rate that is 20 per cent below the national head count rate. Porter and Watts (2017) speak of the various forces that coalesced to produce this success. Orta Martínez, Pellegrini and Arsel (forthcoming) discuss the case of the Achuar community in the Peruvian Amazon, who are seriously adversely affected by the activities of an oil company. They abandoned the strategy of dialogue for one of conflict, according to the authors, including occupying the facilities of the oil company in 2006. One is reminded of Steve Biko's statement, however, when accused of violence by an apartheid-era judge in South Africa: "You and I are now in confrontation, but I see no violence."[4] Thus, the strategy employed by the Peruvian community is more that of confrontation rather than violent conflict.

In the ultimate analysis, the resource curse is neither curse nor destiny, as the title of the volume edited by Lederman and Maloney (2007) suggests.

---

4. See www.southafrica.to/people/Quotes/SteveBiko/SteveBiko.php (accessed 7 February 2018). I am indebted to Fabio Diaz Pabon for drawing my attention to this quote.

Based on the review of the empirical evidence for the resource curse, one can argue that the political resource curse (institutional impact) is more salient than the so-called economic resource curse (effect on growth), and even there the evidence is mixed. The economics and politics are inseparable, however, as growth is affected by the policies chosen in a particular political context. Equally, good or bad economic performance leads to institutional change. Generalizations about the processes of the so-called curse are fraught with danger, and it seems to have been more applicable during certain historical periods, as during the 1970s and 1980s, rather than universally. We must eschew path-dependent views of the resource curse, which suggest that the initial quality of institutions at the time of the advent of resource rents locks the economy into an upward trajectory or downward spiral. Instead, room needs to be created within our analytical frameworks to allow for institutional change. The greatest threat posed by natural resource abundance or dependence is if it delays or retards political and economic structural transformation; equally, strategies to cope with the curse require structural transformation in social relations and policy-making.

APPENDIX 1

Growth collapse with rent-seeking

The model below is closely based on Murshed (2010: chap. 2). The innovative feature of the model is that the macroeconomic collapse that comes from a reduction of the capital stock, hence productivity, has micro-foundations in rent-seeking contests. We begin with a competitive game of rent-seeking in the spirit of Tullock (1967). In this framework, several agents compete for a prize equivalent to a pot of rents in each period that resource revenues are available. The competition to capture this prize, which is akin to a tournament, entails a cost, be that bribery, lobbying expenditure, or whatever. Let P represent the winner-take-all prize that each rent-seeking agent is attempting to seize. This prize corresponds to the contestable or appropriable revenue from resource rents. This does not preclude collusive group behaviour, as long as groups compete with each other. Each agent's probability of success will depend on his own rent-seeking expenditure relative to all others. The expected utility (E) of an agent (i) in a symmetrical setting can take the form

$$E_i = \pi_i P - c_i \qquad (\text{A1.1})$$

where π is the probability of winning, based upon the contest success function, and c represents lobbying costs or expenditures. The contest success function is given by

$$\pi_i(c_i, c_j, s) = \frac{c^s_i}{c^s_1 + c^s_2}; i = 1, 2; j \neq i \qquad (\text{A1.2})$$

In this example above there are only two agents, $i = 1, 2$. The crucial parameter s represents the "efficiency or productivity" of lobbying expenditure or bribery; if $s > 1$, there are increasing returns to scale in such expenditure. If that is so, under weak institutions of governance, when the law is honoured more in the breach than in the keeping, lobbying expenditure is even more productive as far as rent-seekers are concerned. In many ways, s can be characterized to be negatively related to good governance and institutional quality, with $s > 1$ being a sign of a very poor institutional environment. Wick and Bulte (2006) also incorporate increasing returns to scale in connection with resource rents when the agent's choice is between rent-seeking and conflict. My set-up is different: the increasing returns to scale emanate from poor institutional quality and not the mere "pointiness" (concentrated) or capturability of resources. My analysis has some similarities to the grabber-friendly institutions described in Mehlum, Moene and Torvik (2006), but I incorporate increasing returns to scale to that activity, and the possibility of an attrition game. Other theoretical papers in the natural-resource-induced rent-seeking genre do not model the possibility of a variable institutional environment, which may encourage further rent-seeking, although Hodler (2006) considers the effect of rent-seeking (fighting) on property rights. Thus, it is not only that the total available prize (P) determines rent-seeking, but also that the institutional environment may promote further knavery. This is parameterized by s in my model.

Substituting Equation (A1.2) into (A1.1) and maximizing with respect to c_i, we find

$$c_i = \frac{sP}{4}; i = 1, 2 \qquad (A1.3)$$

Equation (A1.3) gives us the Cournot–Nash equilibrium level of lobbying spending by each agent. The substitution of (A1.3) into (A1.1) yields the following expected utility:

$$E_i = \frac{P}{2} - \frac{sP}{4} \qquad (A1.4)$$

The above expression becomes negative if $s > 2$. If this is so, it will lead to an even more socially wasteful war of attrition game, in which the object is to make one's opponents exit the rent-seeking contest because an opponent's very presence yields negative expected utility. It is generally accepted, after

128

Bhagwati (1982), that lobbying or rent-seeking expenditure is almost always wasteful, and here it will detract from the capital stock. Total lobbying expenditures may cause a decline in the capital stock, as investment in capital declines. At this juncture I introduce two definitions that I intend to utilize in the macro-model of growth collapse:

$$\sum c_i = z_0, \text{ and } \cdots P = z_1 \qquad (A1.5)$$

We now turn to the macro-model. The economy is guided by choices made by a representative agent and all variables are represented in per capita values. The equilibrium level of the capital stock in the steady state implicitly defines growth rates, and a fall in the equilibrium capital stock implies a decline in the growth rate. Growth collapses are associated with periods of declining capital accumulation. An "infinitely" lived individual maximizes utility at each time period (t) according to

$$\text{Max } U(t) = \int_t^\infty u(C(t))\exp(-it)\,dt \qquad (A1.6)$$

where utility (U or u) depends on consumption, C; exp is the exponential operator; and the real interest rate is i. Maximization is subject to two budget constraints at t:

$$\dot{D}(t) = C(t) + I(t) + iD(t) - f(k(t)) \qquad (A1.7)$$

$$\dot{k}(t) = I(t) \qquad (A1.8)$$

We ignore the rate of depreciation. Output subject to constant returns, Y, is given by

$$Y(t) = f(k(t)) \qquad (A1.9)$$

The stock constraint, Equation (A1.8), tells us that the rate of capital accumulation at time t is equal to investment (I) at time t. Equation (A1.9) is the production function for Y (output) written in per capita fashion; k is the capital–labour ratio. Equation (A1.7) is the flow constraint in an open economy. It informs us that the rate of accumulation of international debt is given by the excess of consumption (C) plus investment (I) and debt servicing $(iD$, where i is the interest rate and D is the debt stock), over production or output $(f(k))$. This is the exact counterpart of the current account deficit, the excess of absorption (expenditure) over output (income). In the closed economy context, or with no debt, investment is equal to output minus consumption.

In order to subject the system to the effects of a resource boom, we incorporate an additive and multiplicative effect to the production function in (A1.9):

$$Y(t) = (1 - z_0)f(k(t)) + z_1 \qquad \text{(A1.10)}$$

Here z_0 represents the diversion of a part of the capital stock from ordinary production to rent-seeking activities, and z_1 is the revenue component. They are described by Equation (A1.5). The revenue component can be either positive or negative. If, as in the case of some countries, resource revenues are mainly transferred abroad via corruption and other forms of leakage, then z_1 is negative in its effect on the macroeconomy. If it generates income in the domestic economy it is positive. The additive component, z_1, has no effect on the marginal product of capital, and therefore no effect on investment or the capital stock. When positive, it immediately raises consumption, but not savings, by a proportionate amount. Conversely, consumption declines if revenues are negative. Adjustment in income is immediate and dramatic. In an open economy, however, the country might be able to borrow from abroad to smooth consumption, with implications for future indebtedness and debt servicing. Note that the resource rents (z_1) are exogenous in the sense that they are like a pure transfer, or manna from heaven. The costs to the economy (the multiplicative term z_0) are an endogenous outcome of rent-seeking activities, however, described above in Equations (A1.1) to (A1.4).

I now turn to the effects of extracted resource rents on productivity, investment and the capital stock. This occurs via the multiplicative term. We postulate that rent-seeking will reduce the effective marginal product of capital, because of the diversion of productive investment away from normal activities towards rent-seeking, analysed in the rent-seeking contest above.[1]

---

1. For a more detailed derivation, see Murshed (2010: chap. 2).

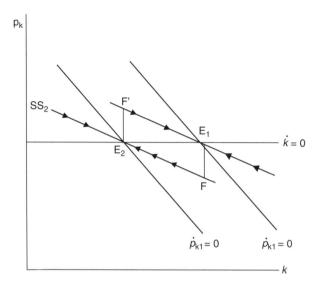

Figure A1.1 Growth collapse

In Figure A1.1 the $\dot{k} = 0$ schedule is a horizontal line. This tells us that the optimal capital stock is related to marginal productivity and not p_k. The $\dot{p}_k = 0$ line is negatively sloped, as a rise in p_k increases the rate of investment, which in turn raises the capital stock (k). With a fixed interest rate and marginal productivity of capital, however, the capital stock is given at its optimal level, k^*, such that $p_k = 1$ in the steady state; hence k will decline.

When there is a negative effect on the capital stock, the economy jumps from the initial equilibrium at E_1 to the new saddle path (SS_2) at point F. The $\dot{p}_k = 0$ schedule will then shift to the left, and the final equilibrium is at E_2. There is an initial, but not steady-state, fall in the shadow price of capital. This makes the rate of investment negative between F and E_2, which, in turn, causes the capital stock to decline, prompting negative growth. The economy comes to a rest with a lower steady-state capital stock and growth rate at E_2. The growth collapse occurs between F and E_2. Net output declines in the new steady state on account of the combined effect of the diversion of output to rent-seeking and a lower capital stock. There is also a decline in consumption associated with lower net output. Rent-seeking expenditure per se is greater the higher the prize, P in Equations (A1.1) to (A1.4) or z_1 in

(A1.10). This implies a large amount of resource rents. But, more importantly, total rent-seeking expenditure for any level of natural resource rents will be greater when the polity is more predatory and oligarchic and poor institutions abound. This means that z_0 is large in (A1.5) and $s > 1$.

In other situations, in which natural resource revenues are more spread out or diffuse, the prize (P) in (A1.1) to (A1.4) could be considerably smaller (say P/n, the population being given by n). Moreover, in societies in which many agents enter the rent-seeking contest, the benefit to each of lobbying expenditure is smaller. In either case, z_0 will be smaller, as $s < 1$, and the resultant negative growth effect is also diminished. A developmental state working with superior institutions that is democratic or benevolent would reduce lobbying and rent-seeking expenditure. Rent-seeking contests would not yield much to corrupt agents, who would be better off in productive entrepreneurial activities. In that case, natural resource revenues would not retard growth ($z_0 = 0$). It would also mean P or z_1 (the resource rents) in (A1.10) would become a part of the regular production process in (A1.9).

APPENDIX 2

A model of civil war with greed and grievances

The model below is closely based on Murshed (2010: chap. 2). There are two sides to the potential conflict: a government side and a rebel group. Both sides have access to resource rents or booty, which could be viewed as the greed motivation for conflict. The rebels have some historical grievances, based on relative deprivation and/or other forms of horizontal inequality against the government, which can be assuaged by a transfer from the government.

The government side

The expected utility of the government side (G) is given by

$$G = \pi(a,e)G^P + (1-\pi)(\cdot)G^C - C(a) \qquad \text{(A2.1)}$$

where G^P and G^C denote utilities or pay-offs in peace and conflict respectively, weighted by the probabilities of the two states, peace (π) and war $(1 - \pi)$. The pay-offs are endogenous in the sense that the probabilities of the two states depend on a strategic action (a) undertaken by the government. The strategic action parameter itself will depend on a number of variables, described below. C is the cost of undertaking peaceful action, a.

Note that the government's income, (Y^G), defined in Equation (A2.2), is greater during peacetime, $\alpha > 1$. This is because income is derived from tax revenues, which in turn are related to output and the technology of production. During wartime rising transactions costs, reduced investment and the flight of labour all combine to reduce output. And output losses are generally greater in resource-diffuse economies than in "point-sourced" ones, since the latter are easier (and more profitable) to defend. But, even in the latter case, there are investments necessary to make extractive mining sectors function. In a state of war, there are certain lootable revenues (X^G) that can be obtained, and these correspond to greed. The parameter a is the strategic choice variable of the government. T is the "transfer" made by the government to the rebels in the state of relative peace and depends on government income. This can take a variety of forms, including broad-based social and development expenditure extended to the rebels. F denotes military expenditure; this is clearly greater in wartime than during peace, hence $c > p$. The amount of F will depend on the objective function of the state (W), and whether or not the war or peace tendency is more dominant within the government. Note that even the peaceful outcome is a state of armed peace, as a minimum credible deterrent is required by the state.

$$G^P = \alpha Y^G - pF^G - T$$
$$\alpha > 1$$
$$G^C = Y^G - cF^G + X^G$$
$$a = \frac{T(Y^G)}{F^G(W)}$$
$$c > p > 0, c + p = 1 \tag{A2.2}$$

The probabilities of the two states are not related to a Tullock-type contest success function, as in Hirshleifer (1995), for example. This is because the low-intensity conflict is not a war of attrition. The rebels cannot expect to oust the government solely via a military victory, and vice versa. Nor does the government have a Weberian monopoly over violence. We are concerned with a continuum of possible states of peace or war.

In fact, the strategic actions of the two players are a ratio of peaceful to belligerent behaviour, and are therefore mixed strategies. This is reflected in the ratio of transfers to military expenditure in the definition of a in (A2.2) for the government. Thus, its strategic action depends on T, Y^G, X^G, W and F^G. Totally differentiating the expression for a in Equation (A2.2), we get

$$da = \frac{T_1}{F^G} dY^G - \frac{T}{F^{G2}_1} dW \tag{A2.3}$$

The first term on the right-hand side of (A2.3) is positive, while the second term has a negative sign before it (T_1, $F^G_1 > 0$). The first term is associated with a transfer to the rebel or excluded group, and the second corresponds to a greater military effort against the rebels. W stands for the government's objective function with respect to military expenditure. The chances of the peaceful state in Equation (A2.1) are positively associated with a. In other words, $\pi_a > 0$, but $\pi_{aa} < 0$, because of diminishing returns. Peace is more likely if a transfer is made by including the excluded, rather than if there is a resort to military expenditure with a view to overthrowing the rebels. There is a trade-off between transfers and fighting to generate the same level of expected utility indicated in (A2.1). A more benevolent and developmental state may prefer making transfers to rebels to fighting them. In Equation (A2.1), C is the cost function of undertaking the action, a, which increases the probability of peace, π. Both $C_a > 0$ and $C_{aa} > 0$. This cost function also incorporates the psychological costs of making peace.

The rebel side

Turning to the rebel or excluded group, its expected utility (R) is given by

$$R = \pi(a,e)R^P + (1-\pi)(\cdot)R^C - E(e) \qquad \text{(A2.4)}$$

where

$$
\begin{aligned}
R^P &= \alpha Y^R - pF^R + T \\
R^C &= Y^R - cF^R + X^R \\
e &= \frac{T(Y^G)}{\theta}
\end{aligned}
$$

$$\text{(A2.5)}$$

The pay-offs are endogenous, in the sense that the probabilities of the two states depend on a strategic action (e) undertaken by the rebels. The strategic action parameter itself will depend on a number of variables, described below. The rebel side's income may be greater during peace, at least for diffuse economies, for the reasons outlined above. The income of the rebel group might be derived from voluntary contributions in rebel areas, coercion of the local population, contributions from sympathetic citizens abroad or the export of narcotics and natural resources such as diamonds, particularly in the state of war (X^R). E is the cost of effort, e, which increases the probability of peace, π. In addition, $\pi_e > 0$, but $\pi_{ee} < 0$, $E_e > 0$ and $E_{ee} > 0$. Peaceful effort increases as more transfers or broad-based social expenditures are extended to the rebel group.

I introduce an exogenous parameter, $\theta > 0$, which affects the level of peaceful action, and captures the horizontal inequality, polarization or relative deprivation dimension. It is based on the grievance measures, and is a non-pecuniary and intrinsic measure of historical and *pure grievance*. Rebel grievances, therefore, contain a pure or historical element (θ) and a component that can be mollified via pecuniary means through broad-based spending (T). This grievance or sense of injustice serves to bind the rebels into a group, overcoming Olson's (1965) collective action problem. Furthermore, the presence of the grievance is what precludes cooperation or an effective social compact between the government and the rebels. A rise in θ could be caused by an increase in poverty or a greater perception of injustice; it serves to increase the cost of peaceful effort and raises belligerency levels among rebels. Alternatively, it could reflect the perceived denial of a fair share of resource rents to the rebel group. Thus, the strategic action by the rebels depends on T and θ. Totally differentiating e in Equation (A2.5) gives

$$de = \frac{T_1}{\theta} dY^G - \frac{T}{\theta^2} d\theta \qquad (A2.6)$$

Thus, peaceful efforts, e, increase with transfers from the state (the first term on the right-hand side of A2.6) and decrease with a rise in grievances (the second term on the right-hand side of A2.6).

Non-cooperative behaviour

Conflict (non-cooperation) occurs because neither side can cooperate or enter into a social contract, because of the presence of historical grievances, low levels of transfers to the rebel group or imperfectly credible transfers to the rebel group or because the returns to peace relative to war are insufficient (greed). In the model, the strategies adopted by the two sides (a and e) in a Cournot–Nash non-cooperative one-shot game are endogenous. This in turn depends on disposable income and war booty (greed); transfers and fighting intensities hinge on the nature of the government as well as pure grievances on the rebel side.

Each side will maximize its own utility with respect to its own choice variable, and set it equal to zero. For the government, it implies maximizing utility in Equation (A2.1) with respect to a, as shown by

$$\frac{\partial G}{\partial a} = \pi_a \left[G^P(\cdot) - G^C(\cdot) \right] - C_a = 0 \qquad (A2.7)$$

The rebels maximize (A2.4) with respect to e:

$$\frac{\partial R}{\partial e} = \pi_e \left[R^P(\cdot) - R^C(\cdot) \right] - E_e = 0 \qquad (A2.8)$$

Equations (A2.7) and (A2.8) form the basis of the reaction functions for both sides, obtained by totally differentiating both with respect to a and e. Thus

$$\frac{de}{da / R^G} = \frac{C_{aa} + \pi_{aa} \left[G^C(\cdot) - G^P(\cdot) \right]}{\pi_{ae} \left[G^P(\cdot) - G^C(\cdot) \right]} \gtreqless 0 \; if \; \pi_{ae} \gtreqless 0 \qquad (A2.9)$$

$$\frac{de}{da / R^R} = \frac{\pi_{ae} \left[R^P(\cdot) - R^C(\cdot) \right]}{E_{ee} + \pi_{ee} \left[R^C(\cdot) - R^P(\cdot) \right]} \gtreqless 0 \; if \; \pi_{ae} \gtreqless 0 \qquad (A2.10)$$

Note that $\pi_{ae} = \pi_{ea}$ by symmetry.

The reaction functions are positively sloped if $\pi_{ae} > 0$, implying that the two strategies are complements (see Figure A2.1). This is the standard assumption in the literature on conflict; see, for example, Hirshleifer (1995). It means that increases in fighting or peaceful efforts by one side are matched in the same direction by the other side. In our model, however, we allow for the possibility that $\pi_{ae} < 0$, the choice variables are strategic substitutes, and the reaction functions could slope downwards (Figure A2.2). This can occur only because the strategy space is defined in terms of peace. Thus, if one side behaves more peacefully, it increases the utility of both parties, and the other side may free-ride on this action by actually reducing its own action. Recall that we are concerned with relative states of war and peace. Thus, the two strategies can become substitutes the closer society is to complete peace, or the lower the state of belligerency. The higher the intensity of war, the greater the likelihood of the two strategies being complements (Figure A2.1), as is conventional in the literature.

A rise in booty (greed)

This raises the gains from conflict in the presence of a natural-resource- or narcotics-based economic boom generating rents. In Figures A2.1 and A2.2 we consider the rise in available war loot, bearing in mind that this increase could be relevant to either side or both sides. Figure A2.1 represents the case when the two strategies are complements. An increase in available booty to the government (X^G) shifts its reaction function leftwards, indicating a lower optimal choice of a for any level of e. For the rebel group, a greater availability of lootable resources (X^R) has the effect of a downward shift in its reaction function, pointing to reduced e for every level of a. When both sides have equal access to booty, the shift is to point B, with an obvious decline in activities to promote peace. When it is exclusive to the government, point G becomes applicable; when it is only the rebels, point R is the new equilibrium. The side receiving the booty lowers its action or effort accompanied by a corresponding, but less than proportionate, decline in its opponent's strategic variable.

A qualitatively different picture emerges in Figure A2.2, where the strategies are substitutes. Greater loot shifts reaction functions in a downward direction. Here the greater endowment of booty by one side exclusively not only reduces its incentive to undertake its own relevant strategic action or effort but also causes it to shift part of the burden of peaceful behaviour to its opponent. In general, the greater availability of booty or lootable resources to both sides (as opposed to one side only) reduces the equilibrium levels of peaceful behaviour, as illustrated by point B in Figures A2.1 and A2.2.

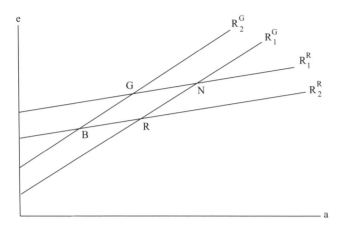

Figure A2.1 Booty (complements)

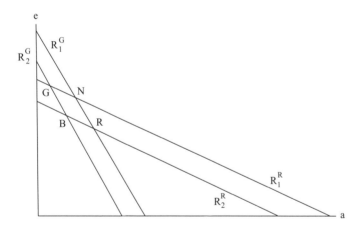

Figure A2.2 Booty (substitutes)

References

Acemoglu, D., S. Johnson & J. Robinson 2001. "The Colonial Origins of Comparative Development: An Empirical Investigation". *American Economic Review* 91 (5): 1369–401.

Acemoglu, D., S. Johnson & J. Robinson 2002. "Reversal of Fortune: Geography and Institutions in the Making of the Modern World Income Distribution". *Quarterly Journal of Economics* 117 (4): 1231–44.

Acemoglu, D., S. Johnson & J. Robinson 2003. "An African Success Story: Botswana". In *In Search of Prosperity: Analytic Narratives on Economic Growth*, D. Rodrik (ed.), 80–119. Princeton, NJ: Princeton University Press.

Acemoglu, D., S. Johnson & J. Robinson 2005. "Institutions as the Fundamental Cause of Long-Run Growth". In *Handbook of Economic Growth*, vol. 1A, P. Aghion & S. Durlauf (eds), 385–472. Amsterdam: Elsevier.

Acemoglu, D. & J. Robinson 2006. "Economic Backwardness in Political Perspective". *American Political Science Review* 100 (1): 115–31.

Acemoglu, D. & J. Robinson 2009. *Economic Origins of Dictatorship and Democracy*. Cambridge: Cambridge University Press.

Ahmadov, A. 2014. "Oil, Democracy and Context: A Meta-Analysis". *Comparative Political Studies* 47 (9): 1238–367.

Ajakaiye, O., P. Collier & A. Ekpo 2011. "Management of Resource Revenue: Nigeria". In *Plundered Nations? Successes and Failures in Natural Resource Extraction*, P. Collier & T. Venables (eds), 231–61. Basingstoke: Palgrave Macmillan.

Akerlof, G. & R. Kranton 2000. "Economics and Identity". *Quarterly Journal of Economics* 115 (3): 715–53.

Allcott, H. & D. Keniston 2014. "Dutch Disease or Agglomeration? The Local Economic Effects of Natural Resource Booms in Modern America", Working Paper 20508. Cambridge, MA: National Bureau of Economic Research.

Amoako-Tuffour, J. 2016. "Should Countries Invest Resource Revenues Abroad When Demands for Public Infrastructure Are Pressing at Home? The Dilemma of Sovereign Wealth Funds in Sub-Saharan Africa". *Journal of African Economies* 25 (AERC Supplement 2): 41–58.

Andersen, J. & S. Aslaksen 2008. "Constitutions and the Resource Curse". *Journal of Development Economics* 87 (2): 227–46.

Andersen, J. & M. Ross 2014. "The Big Oil Change: A Closer Look at the Haber–Menaldo Analysis". *Comparative Political Studies* 47 (7): 993–1021.

Apergis, N. & J. Payne 2014. "The Oil Curse, Institutional Quality and Growth in MENA Countries: Evidence from Time-Varying Cointegration". *Energy Economics* 46 (C): 1–9.

Aragón, F. & J. Rud 2013. "Natural Resources and Local Communities: Evidence from a Peruvian Gold Mine". *American Economic Journal: Economic Policy* 5 (2): 1–25.

Arzeki, R. & M. Brückner 2011. "Oil Rents, Corruption and State Stability". *European Economic Review* 55 (7): 955–63.

Arezki, R. & A. Sy 2016. "Financing Africa's Infrastructure Deficit: From Development Banking to Long-Term Investing". *Journal of African Economies* 2 (AERC Supplement 2): 59–73.

Asher, S. & P. Novosad 2013. "Digging for Development: Natural Resource Wealth, Mining Booms and Local Economic Development in India". Available at: http://sites.bu.edu/neudc/files/2014/10/paper_241.pdf (accessed 30 April 2018).

Aslaksen, S. 2010. "Oil and Democracy: More than a Cross-Country Correlation". *Journal of Peace Research* 47 (4): 421–31.

Aslaksen, S. & R. Torvik 2006. "A Theory of Civil Conflict and Democracy in Rentier States". *Scandinavian Journal of Economics* 108 (4): 571–85.

Auty, R. 1993. *Sustaining Development in Mineral Economies: The Resource Curse Thesis*. London: Routledge.

Auty, R. 1997. "Natural Resources, the State and Development Strategy". *Journal of International Development* 9 (4): 651–63.

Auty, R. 2001. "A Growth Collapse with High Rent Point Resources: Saudi Arabia". In *Resource Abundance and Economic Development*, R. Auty (ed.), 193–207. Oxford: Oxford University Press.

Auty, R. 2007. "Natural Resources, Capital Accumulation and the Resource Curse". *Ecological Economics* 61 (4): 627–34.

Auty, R. & J. Evia 2001. "A Growth Collapse with Point Resources: Bolivia". In *Resource Abundance and Economic Development*, R. Auty (ed.), 179–92. Oxford: Oxford University Press.

Auty, R. & A. Gelb 2001. "Political Economy of Resource-Abundant States". In *Resource Abundance and Economic Development*, R. Auty (ed.), 126–44. Oxford: Oxford University Press.

Badeeb, R., H. Lean & J. Clark 2017. "The Evolution of the Natural Resource Curse Thesis: A Critical Literature Survey". *Resources Policy* 51: 123–34.

Baland, J. & P. Francois 2000. "Rent-Seeking and Resource Booms". *Journal of Development Economics* 61 (2): 527–42.

Baldwin, R. 1956. "Patterns of Development in Newly Settled Regions". *Manchester School* 24 (2): 161–79.

Barnett, S. & R. Ossowski 2003. "Operational Aspects of Fiscal Policies in Oil-Producing Countries". In *Fiscal Policy Formulation and Implementation in Oil-Producing Countries*, J. Davis, R. Ossowski & A. Fedelino (eds), 45–82. Washington, DC: International Monetary Fund.

Bazzi, S. & C. Blattman 2014. "Economic Shocks and Conflict: Evidence from Commodity Prices". *American Economic Journal: Macroeconomics* 6 (4): 1–38.

Berman, N., M. Couttenier, D. Rohner & M. Thoenig 2017. "This Mine is Mine! How Minerals Fuel Conflicts in Africa". *American Economic Review* 107 (6): 1564–1610.

Bhagwati, J. 1982. "Directly Unproductive, Profit-seeking (DUP) Activities. *Journal of Political Economy* 90 (5): 988–1002.

Bhattacharya, S. & P. Collier 2014. "Public Capital in Resource Rich Countries: Is There a Curse?". *Oxford Economic Papers* 66 (1): 1–24.

Bhattacharya, S. & R. Hodler 2010. "Natural Resources, Democracy and Corruption". *European Economic Review* 54 (4): 608–21.

Bhattacharya, S. & R. Hodler 2014. "Do Natural Resource Revenues Hinder Financial Development? The Role of Political Institutions". *World Development* 57 (C): 101–13.

Birdsall, N., T. Pinckney & R. Sabot 2001. "Natural Resources, Human Capital and Growth". In *Resource Abundance and Economic Development*, R. Auty (ed.), 57–75. Oxford: Oxford University Press.

Blanco, L., K. O'Connor & J. Nugent 2016. "Does Oil Hinder Democratic Development? A Time-Series Analysis", Working Paper 61. Malibu, CA: Pepperdine University, School of Public Policy.

Boadway, R. & M. Keen 2008. "Theoretical Perspectives on Resource Tax Design". Mimeo, International Monetary Fund.

Bornhorst, F., J. Thornton & S. Gupta 2008. "Natural Resource Endowments, Governance and the Domestic Revenue Effect: Evidence from a Panel of Countries", Working Paper 08/170. Washington, DC: International Monetary Fund.

Boschini, A., J. Petterson & J. Roine 2013. "The Resource Curse and Its Potential Reversal". *World Development* 43 (1): 19–41.

Bourguignon, F. & T. Verdier 2000. "Oligarchy, Democracy, Inequality and Growth". *Journal of Development Economics* 62 (2): 285–313.

Brouder, A. 2009. "Extractive Industries Transparency Initiative". In *Handbook of Transnational Economic Governance Regimes*, C. Titje & A. Brouder (eds), 849–64. Leiden: Brill.

Brown, G. 2005. "Horizontal Inequalities, Ethnic Separatism, and Violent Conflict: The Case of Aceh, Indonesia". Background paper for *Human Development Report*, United Nations Development Programme.

Brückner, M. & A. Ciccone 2010. "International Commodity Prices, Growth and the Outbreak of Civil War in Sub-Saharan Africa". *Economic Journal* 120 (544): 519–34.

Brunnschweiler, C. & E. Bulte 2008. "The Resource Curse Revisited and Revised: A Tale of Paradoxes and Red Herrings". *Journal of Environmental Economics and Management* 55 (3): 248–64.

Brunnschweiler, C. & E. Bulte 2009. "Natural Resources and Violent Conflict: Resource Abundance, Dependence and the Onset of Civil Wars". *Oxford Economic Papers* 61 (4): 651–74.

Bueno de Mesquita, B., A. Smith, R. Siverson & J. Morrow 2003. *The Logic of Political Survival*. Cambridge, MA: MIT Press.

Buhaug, H. & J. Rød 2006. "Local Determinants of African Civil Wars, 1970–2001". *Political Geography* 25 (3): 315–35.

Bulte, E. & R. Damania 2008. "Resources for Sale: Corruption, Democracy and the Resource Curse". *B.E. Journal of Economic Analysis and Policy* 8 (1): article 5.

Busse, M. & S. Gröning 2013. "The Resource Curse Revisited: Governance and Natural Resources". *Public Choice* 154 (1): 1–20.

Caselli, F. & T. Cunningham 2007. "Political Decision Making in Resource Abundant Countries". Paper presented at the Oxford Centre for the Analysis of Resource Rich Economies annual conference, University of Oxford, 14 December.

Caselli, F. & G. Michaels 2013. "Do Oil Windfalls Improve Living Standards? Evidence from Brazil". *American Economic Journal: Applied Economics* 5 (1): 208–38.

Caselli, F. & A. Tesei 2016. "Resource Windfalls, Political Regimes and Political Stability". *Review of Economics and Statistics* 98 (3): 573–90.

Cederman, L.-E., K.-S. Gleditsch & H. Buhaug 2013. *Inequality, Grievances, and Civil War*. New York: Cambridge University Press.

Chenery, H. 1979. *Structural Change and Development Policy*. Washington, DC: Oxford University Press for the World Bank.

Chichilnisky, G. 1994. "North–South Trade and the Global Environment". *American Economic Review* 84 (4): 851–74.

Clarida, R. & R. Findlay 1992. "Government, Trade and Comparative Advantage". *American Economic Review* 82 (2): 122–7.

Clark, C. 1940. *The Conditions of Economic Progress*, 3rd edn. London: Macmillan.

Cockx, L. & N. Francken 2016. "Natural Resources: A Curse on Education Spending?". *Energy Policy* 92 (C): 394–408.

Collier, P. & B. Goderis 2007. "Commodity Prices, Growth, and the Natural Resource Curse: Reconciling a Conundrum", Working Paper 2007-15. Oxford: University of Oxford, Centre for the Study of African Economies.

Collier, P. & A. Hoeffler 2004. "Greed and Grievance in Civil Wars". *Oxford Economic Papers* 56 (4): 563–95.

Collier, P. & A. Hoeffler 2009. "Testing the Neocon Agenda: Democracy in Resource-Rich Societies". *European Economic Review* 53 (3): 293–308.

Collier, P., A. Hoeffler & D. Rohner 2009. "Beyond Greed and Grievance: Feasibility and Civil War". *Oxford Economic Papers* 61 (1): 1–27.

Collier, P., A. Hoeffler & M. Söderbom 2004. "On the Duration of Civil War". *Journal of Peace Research* 41 (3): 253–73.

Cornia, A. (ed.) 2014. *Falling Inequality in Latin America: Policy Changes and Lessons*. Oxford: Oxford University Press.

Cotet, A. & K. Tsui 2013. "Oil and Conflict: What Does the Cross Country Evidence Really Show?". *American Economic Journal: Macroeconomics* 5 (1): 49–80.

Cramton, P. 2007. "How Best to Auction Oil Rights". In *Escaping the Resource Curse*, M. Humphreys, J. Sachs & J. Stiglitz (eds), 114–51. New York: Columbia University Press.

Cumming, D., G. Wood, I. Filatotchev & J. Reinecke (eds) 2017. *Oxford Handbook of Sovereign Wealth Funds*. Oxford: Oxford University Press.

Cust, J. 2015. "The Spatial Effects of Resource Extraction: Mining in Indonesia", discussion paper. Oxford: University of Oxford, Centre for the Analysis of Resource Rich Economies.

Cust, J. & C. Viale 2016. "Is There Evidence for a Subnational Resource Curse?", policy paper. New York: Natural Resource Governance Institute.

Dal Bó, E. & P. Dal Bó 2011. "Workers, Warriors and Criminals: Social Conflict in General Equilibrium". *Journal of the European Economics Association* 9 (4): 646–77.

Deacon, R. 2011. "The Political Economy of the Resource Curse: A Survey of Theory and Evidence". *Foundations and Trends in Microeconomics* 7 (2): 111–208.

De Soysa, I. 2002. "Paradise Is a Bazaar? Testing the Effects of Greed, Creed, Grievance and Governance on Civil War, 1989–1999". *Journal of Peace Research* 39 (4): 395–416.

De Soysa, I. & E. Neumayer 2007. "Resource Wealth and the Risk of Civil War Onset: Results from a New Dataset on Natural Resource Rents, 1970–99". *Conflict Management and Peace Science* 24 (3): 201–18.

Drelichman, M. 2005. "The Curse of Moctezuma: American Silver and the Dutch Disease". *Explorations in Economic History* 42 (3): 349–80.

Dube, O. & J. Vargas 2013. "Commodity Price Shocks and Civil Conflict: Evidence from Colombia". *Review of Economic Studies* 80 (4): 1384–421.

Dunning, T. 2005. "Resource Dependence, Economic Performance, and Political Stability". *Journal of Conflict Resolution* 49 (4): 451–82.

Easterly, W. 2007. "Inequality Does Cause Underdevelopment". *Journal of Development Economics* 84 (2): 755–76.

Easterly, W. & R. Levine 2003. "Tropics, Germs and Crops: How Endowments Influence Economic Development". *Journal of Monetary Economics* 50 (1): 3–39.

Edgeworth, F. 1881. *Mathematical Psychics: An Essay on the Application of Mathematics to the Moral Sciences.* London: Kegan Paul.

Fearon, J. 2004. "Why Do Some Civil Wars Last So Much Longer than Others?". *Journal of Peace Research* 41 (3): 379–414.

Fearon, J. 2005. "Primary Commodity Exports and Civil War". *Journal of Conflict Resolution* 49 (4): 483–507.

Fearon, J. & D. Laitin 2003. "Ethnicity, Insurgency and Civil War". *American Political Science Review* 97 (1): 75–90.

Ffrench-Davis, R. & R. Devlin 1995. "The Great Latin American Debt Crisis: A Decade of Asymmetric Adjustment". In *Poverty, Prosperity and the World Economy: Essays in Memory of Sidney Dell*, G. Helleiner, S. Abrahamian, E. Bacha, R. Lawrence & P. Malan (eds), 43–80. London: Macmillan.

Fielding, D. & F. Gibson 2013. "Aid and Dutch Disease in Sub-Saharan Africa". *Journal of African Economies* 22 (1):1–21.

Findlay, R. & M. Lundahl 1994. "Natural Resources, 'Vent-for-Surplus' and the Staples Theory". In *From Classical Economics to Development Economics*, G. Meir (ed.), 68–93. New York: St. Martin's Press.

Findlay, R. & M. Lundahl 1999. "Resource Led Growth – A Long Term Perspective: The Relevance of the 1870–1914 Experience for Today's Developing Economies", Working Paper 162. Helsinki: United Nations University, World Institute for Development Economics Research. Available at: www.wider.unu.edu/sites/default/files/wp162.pdf (accessed 21 September 2017).

Findlay, R. & C. Rodriguez 1977. "Intermediate Inputs and Macroeconomic Policy under Flexible Exchange Rates". *Canadian Journal of Economics* 10 (2): 209–17.

Fisher, I. 1906. *The Nature of Capital and Income.* London: Macmillan.

Frankel, J. 2012. "The Natural Resource Curse: A Survey of Diagnoses and Some Prescriptions". In *Commodity Price Volatility and Inclusive Growth in Low-Income Countries*, R. Arezki, C. Pattillo, M. Quintyn & M. Zhu (eds), 7–34. Washington, DC: International Monetary Fund.

Frynas, J. 2017. "Sovereign Wealth Funds and the Resource Curse: Resource Funds and Governance in Resource-Rich Countries". In *Oxford Handbook of Sovereign Wealth Funds*, D. Cumming, G. Wood, I. Filatotchev & J. Reinecke (eds), 123–42. Oxford: Oxford University Press.

Fuentes, R. 2011. "Learning How to Manage Natural Resource Revenue: The Experience of Copper in Chile". In *Plundered Nations? Successes and Failures in Natural Resource Extraction*, P. Collier & T. Venables (eds), 79–113. Basingstoke: Palgrave Macmillan.

Gallup, J., J. Sachs & A. Mellinger 1998. "Geography and Economic Development", Working Paper 6849. Cambridge, MA: National Bureau of Economic Research.

Gelb, A., S. Tordo & H. Halland with N. Arfaa & G. Smith 2014. "Sovereign Wealth Funds and Long-Term Development Finance: Risks and Opportunities", Policy Research Working Paper 6776. Washington, DC: World Bank.

Gilberthorpe, E. & E. Papyrakis 2017. "The Extractive Industries and Development: The Resource Curse at the Micro, Meso and Macro Levels". *Extractive Industries and Society* 2 (2): 381–90.

Gilberthorpe, E. & D. Rajak 2017. "The Anthropology of Extraction: Critical Perspectives on the Resource Curse". *Journal of Development Studies* 53 (2): 186–204.

Glaeser, E., R. La Porta, F. Lopez-de-Silanes & A. Shleifer 2004. "Do Institutions Cause Growth?". *Journal of Economic Growth* 9 (3): 271–303.

Grossman, H. 1991. "A General Equilibrium Model of Insurrections". *American Economic Review* 81 (4): 912–21.

Gurr, T. 1970. *Why Men Rebel*. Princeton, NJ: Princeton University Press.

Gylfason, T. 2001. "Natural Resources, Education and Economic Development". *European Economic Review* 45 (4/6): 847–59.

Haber, S. & V. Menaldo 2011. "Do Natural Resources Fuel Authoritarianism? A Reappraisal of the Resource Curse". *American Political Science Review* 105 (1): 1–24.

Haberly, D. 2017. "From Financialization to Vulture Developmentalism: South–North Strategic Sovereign Wealth Fund Investment and the Politics of the 'Quadruple Bottom Line'". In *Oxford Handbook of Sovereign Wealth Funds*, D. Cumming, G. Wood, I. Filatotchev & J. Reinecke (eds), 87–122. Oxford: Oxford University Press.

Hanley, N., L. Dupuy & E. McLaughlin 2015. "Genuine Savings and Sustainability". *Journal of Economic Surveys* 29 (4): 779–806.

Hartwick, J. 1977. "Intergenerational Equity and the Investing of Rents from Exhaustible Resources". *American Economic Review* 67 (5): 972–4.

Hasson, J. 1956. "Economic Stabilization in a Primary Producing Country". *Journal of Political Economy* 64 (3): 226–41.

Havránek, T., R. Horváth & A. Zeynalov 2016. "Natural Resources and Economic Growth: A Meta-Analysis", Working Paper 1/2016. Prague: Czech National Bank.

Hirschman, A. 1958. *The Strategy of Economic Development*. New Haven, CT: Yale University Press.

Hirshleifer, J. 1995. "Anarchy and Its Breakdown". *Journal of Political Economy* 103 (1): 26–52.

Hodler, R. 2006. "The Curse of Natural Resources in Fractionalized Countries". *European Economic Review* 50 (6): 1367–86.

Hotelling, H. 1931. "The Economics of Exhaustible Resources". *Journal of Political Economy* 40 (4): 137–75.

Humphreys, M. 2005. "Natural Resources, Conflict, and Conflict Resolution: Uncovering the Mechanisms". *Journal of Conflict Resolution* 49 (4): 508–37.

ICG 2006. "Fuelling the Niger Delta Crisis", Africa Report 118. Brussels: International Crisis Group.

Innis, H. 1930. *The Fur Trade in Canada: An Introduction to Canadian Economic History*. New Haven, CT: Yale University Press.

IMF 2012. "Macroeconomic Policy Frameworks for Resource-Rich Developing Countries", Background Paper 1 – Supplement 1. Washington, DC: International Monetary Fund.

IMF 2015. "Saudi Arabia: Selected Issues", Country Report 15/286. Washington, DC: International Monetary Fund.

IMF 2017a. "Botswana: Selected Issues", Country Report 17/250. Washington, DC: International Monetary Fund.

IMF 2017b. "Saudi Arabia: Selected Issues", Country Report 17/317. Washington, DC: International Monetary Fund.

Isham, J., M. Woolcock, L. Pritchett & G. Busby 2005. "The Varieties of Resource Experience: Natural Resource Export Structures and the Political Economy of Economic Growth". *World Bank Economic Review* 19 (2): 141–74.

Jomo, K. 1990. *Growth and Structural Change in the Malaysian Economy*. London: Macmillan.

Jomo, K. & W. Hui 2003. "The Political Economy of Malaysian Federalism: Economic Development, Public Policy and Conflict Containment". *Journal of International Development* 15 (4): 441–56.

Karl, T. 1999. "The Perils of the Petro-State: Reflections on the Paradox of Plenty". *Journal of International Affairs* 53 (1): 31–52.

Kaufmann, D., A. Kraay & M. Mastruzzi 2006. "Governance Matters V: Aggregate and Individual Governance Indicators for 1996–2005", Policy Research Working Paper 4012. Washington, DC: World Bank.

Kim, D. & S. Lin 2017. "Natural Resources and Economic Development: New Panel Evidence". *Environmental Resource Economics* 66 (2): 363–91.

Kolstad, I. 2009. "The Resource Curse: Which Institutions Matter?". *Applied Economics Letters* 16 (4): 439–42.

Krugman, P. 1987. "The Narrow Moving Band, the Dutch Disease and the Competitive Consequences of Mrs Thatcher: Notes on Trade in the Presence of Dynamic Scale Economies". *Journal of Development Economics* 27 (1/2): 41–55.

Lane, P. & A. Tornell 1996. "Power, Growth and the Voracity Effect". *Journal of Economic Growth* 1 (2): 213–41.

Lartey, E., F. Mandelman & P. Acosta 2012. "Remittances, Exchange Rate Regimes and the Dutch Disease: A Panel Data Analysis". *Review of International Economics* 20 (2): 377–95.

Lederman, D. & W. Maloney 2007. *Natural Resources: Neither Curse nor Destiny.* Palo Alto, CA: Stanford University Press for the World Bank.

Lei, Y.-H. & G. Michaels 2014. "Do Giant Oilfield Discoveries Fuel Internal Armed Conflicts?". *Journal of Development Economics* 110 (C): 139–57.

Lewin, M. 2011. "Botswana's Success: Good Governance, Good Policies, and Good Luck". In *Yes Africa Can: Success Stories from a Dynamic Continent*, P. Chuhan-Pole & M. Angwafo (eds), 81–90. Washington, DC: World Bank.

Lewis, W. 1954. "Economic Development with Unlimited Supplies of Labour". *Manchester School* 22 (2): 139–91.

Lind, J., K. Moene & F. Willumsen 2014. "Opium for the Masses? Conflict-Induced Narcotics Production in Afghanistan". *Review of Economics and Statistics* 96 (5): 949–66.

Lujala, P. 2009. "Deadly Combat over Natural Resources: Gems, Petroleum, Drugs and the Severity of Armed Civil Conflict". *Journal of Conflict Resolution* 53 (1): 50–71.

Lujala, P., N. Gleditsch & E. Gilmore 2005. "A Diamond Curse? Civil War and a Lootable Resource". *Journal of Conflict Resolution* 49 (4): 538–62.

Lujala, P., J. Rød & N. Thieme 2007. "Fighting over Oil: Introducing a New Dataset". *Conflict Management and Peace Science* 24 (3): 239–56.

Matsen, E. & R. Torvik 2005. "Optimal Dutch Disease". *Journal of Development Economics* 78 (2): 494–515.

Matsuyama, K. 1992. "Agricultural Productivity, Comparative Advantage and Economic Growth". *Journal of Economic Theory* 58 (2): 317–34.

Mavrotas, G., S. Murshed & S. Torres 2011. "Natural Resource Dependence and Economic Performance in the 1970–2000 Period". *Review of Development Economics* 15 (1): 124–38.

Mehlum, H., K. Moene & R. Torvik 2006. "Institutions and the Resource Curse". *Economic Journal* 116 (508): 1–20.

Mehrara, M. 2009. "Reconsidering the Resource Curse in Oil-Exporting Countries". *Energy Policy* 37 (3): 1165–9.

Meijia, P. & V. Castel 2012. "Could Oil Shine like Diamonds? How Botswana Avoided the Resource Curse and Its Implications for a New Libya", economic brief. Abidjan: African Development Bank. Available at: www.afdb.org/en/news-and-events/could-oil-shine-like-diamonds-how-botswana-avoided-the-resource-curse-and-its-implications-for-a-new-libya-9979 (accessed 30 April 2018).

Metcalfe, R. 2007. "The Natural Resource Curse: An Unequivocal Hypothesis". Mimeo, Imperial College London.

Michaels, G. 2011. "The Long Term Consequences of Resource-Based Specialisation". *Economic Journal* 121 (551): 31–57.

Mintz, J. & D. Chen 2012. "Capturing Economic Rents from Resources through Royalties and Taxes", Research Paper 5 (30). Calgary: University of Calgary, School of Public Policy.

Montalvo, J. & M. Reynal-Querol 2005. "Ethnic Polarization, Potential Conflict, and Civil Wars". *American Economic Review* 95 (3): 796–816.

Moradbeigi, M. & S. Law 2016. "Growth Volatility and the Resource Curse: Does Financial Development Dampen the Oil Shocks?". *Resources Policy* 48: 97–103.

Mosley, P. 2017. *Fiscal Policy and the Natural Resources Curse: How to Escape from the Poverty Trap*. Abingdon: Routledge.

Murphy, K., A. Shleifer & R. Vishny 1991. "The Allocation of Talent: Implications for Growth". *Quarterly Journal of Economics* 106 (2): 503–30.

Murshed, S. 1997. *Macroeconomics for Open Economies*. London: Dryden Press.

Murshed, S. 1999. "A Macroeconomic Model of a Developing Country Endowed with a Natural Resource", Working Paper 165. Helsinki: United Nations University, World Institute for Development Economics Research. Available at: www.wider.unu.edu/sites/default/files/wp165.pdf (accessed 30 April 2018).

Murshed, S. 2001. "Short-Run Models of Natural Resource Endowment". In *Resource Abundance and Economic Development*, R. Auty (ed.), 113–25. Oxford: Oxford University Press.

Murshed, S. 2004. "When Does Natural Resource Abundance Lead to a Resource Curse?", Environmental Economics Programme Discussion Paper 04–01. London: International Institute for Environment and Development. Available at: http://pubs.iied.org/pdfs/9250IIED.pdf (accessed 30 April 2018).

Murshed, S. 2008. "Peacebuilding and Conflict Resolution Strategies in Africa". Background paper for the African Development Bank's annual report.

Murshed, S. 2010. *Explaining Civil War: A Rational Choice Approach*. Cheltenham: Edward Elgar.

Murshed, S. & L. Serino 2011. "The Pattern of Specialization and Economic Growth: The Resource Curse Hypothesis Revisited". *Structural Change and Economic Dynamics* 22 (2): 151–61.

Murshed, S., M. Badiuzzaman & M. Pulok 2015. "Revisiting the Role of the Resource Curse in Shaping Institutions and Growth", Working Paper 605. The Hague: Institute of Social Studies. Available at: http://hdl.handle.net/1765/77766 (accessed 30 April 2018).

Myint, H. 1958. "The 'Classical Theory' of International Trade and the Under-developed Countries". *Economic Journal* 68 (270): 317–37.

Neary, J. & S. van Wijnbergen 1986. "Natural Resources and the Macroeconomy: A Theoretical Framework". In *Natural Resources and the Macroeconomy*, J. Neary & S. van Wijnbergen (eds), 13–45. Oxford: Blackwell.

Norman, C. 2009. "Rule of Law and the Resource Curse: Abundance versus Intensity". *Environmental and Resource Economics* 43 (2): 183–207.

OECD 2017. "Policy Dialogue on Natural Resource-Based Development: Work Stream 2 – Revenue Spending and Natural Resource Funds". Paris: Organisation for Economic Co-operation and Development.

Olson, M. 1965. *The Logic of Collective Action: Public Goods and the Theory of Groups*. Cambridge, MA: Harvard University Press.

Olson, M. 1996. "Big Bills Left on the Sidewalk: Why Some Nations Are Rich, and Others Poor". *Journal of Economic Perspectives* 10 (1): 3–24.

Orta Martínez, M., L. Pellegrini & M. Arsel (forthcoming). "'The Squeaky Wheel Gets the Grease'? The 'Conflict Imperative' and the Slow Fight against Environmental Injustice in Northern Peruvian Amazon". *Ecology and Society*.

Paler, L. 2013. "Keeping the Public Purse: An Experiment in Windfalls, Taxes, and the Incentives to Restrain Government". *American Political Science Review* 107 (4): 706–25.

Palma, J. 2014. "Industrialization, 'Premature' Deindustrialization and the Dutch Disease". *Revista NECAT* 3 (5): 3–32.

Papyrakis, E. 2017. "The Resource Curse – What Have We Learned from Two Decades of Intensive Research: Introduction to the Special Issue". *Journal of Development Studies* 53 (2): 175–85.

Papyrakis, E. & R. Gerlagh 2007. "Resource Abundance and Economic Growth in the United States". *European Economic Review* 51 (4): 1011–39.

Papyrakis, E. & O. Raveh 2014. "An Empirical Analysis of a Regional Dutch Disease: The Case of Canada". *Environmental and Resource Economics* 58 (2): 179–98.

Papyrakis, E., M. Rieger & E. Gilberthorpe 2017. "Corruption and the Extractive Industries Transparency Initiative". *Journal of Development Studies* 53 (2): 295–309.

Perälä, M. 2000. "Explaining Growth Failures: Natural Resource Type and Growth". Mimeo, United Nations University, World Institute for Development Economics Research.

Pérez Ruiz, E. 2017. "Mining Spillovers in Chile", Working Paper 17/177. Washington, DC: International Monetary Fund.

Pinto, B. 1987. "Nigeria during and after the Oil Boom: A Policy Comparison with Indonesia". *World Bank Economic Review* 1 (3): 419–45.

Porter, D. & M. Watts 2017. "Righting the Resource Curse: Institutional Politics and State Capabilities in Edo State, Nigeria". *Journal of Development Studies* 53 (2): 249–63.

Poteete, A. 2009. "Is Development Path Dependent or Political? A Reinterpretation of Mineral-Dependent Development in Botswana". *Journal of Development Studies* 45 (4): 544–71.

Prebisch, R. 1950. *The Economic Development of Latin America and Its Principal Problems*. New York: United Nations.

Pritchett, L. 1997. "Divergence, Big Time". *Journal of Economic Perspectives* 11 (3): 3–17.

Ramady, M. 2005. *The Saudi Arabian Economy: Policies, Achievements and Challenges*. New York: Springer.

Rawls, J. 1971. *A Theory of Justice*. Cambridge, MA: Harvard University Press.

Robinson, J. & R. Torvik 2005. "White Elephants". *Journal of Public Economics* 89 (2/3): 197–210.

Robinson, J., T. Verdier & R. Torvik 2006. "Political Foundations of the Resource Curse". *Journal of Development Economics* 79 (2): 447–68.

Rodrik, D. 1999. "Where Did All the Growth Go? External Shocks, Social Conflict, and Growth Collapses". *Journal of Economic Growth* 4 (4): 385–412.

Rodrik, D. 2016. "Premature Deindustrialization". *Journal of Economic Growth* 21 (1): 1–32.

Rodrik, D., A. Subramanian & F. Trebbi 2004. "Institutions Rule: The Primacy of Institutions over Geography and Integration in Economic Development". *Journal of Economic Growth* 9 (2): 131–65.

Romer, P. 1990. "Endogenous Technological Change". *Journal of Political Economy* 98 (5): S71–S102.

Ross, M. 2001. "Does Oil Hinder Democracy?". *World Politics* 53 (3): 325–61.

Ross, M. 2003. "Oil, Drugs and Diamonds: The Varying Role of Natural Resources in Civil Wars". In *The Political Economy of Armed Conflict: Beyond Greed and Grievance*, K. Ballentine & J. Sherman (eds), 47–70. Boulder, CO: Lynne Rienner.

Ross, M. 2004a. "Does Taxation Lead to Representation?". *British Journal of Political Science* 34 (2): 229–49.

Ross, M. 2004b. "What Do We Know about Natural Resources and Civil Wars?". *Journal of Peace Research* 41 (3): 337–56.

Ross, M. 2006. "A Closer Look at Oil, Diamond and Civil War". *Annual Review of Political Science* 9: 265–300.

Ross, M. 2008. "Oil, Islam and Women". *American Political Science Review* 102 (1): 107–23.

Sachs, J. 1999. "Resource Endowments and the Real Exchange Rate: A Comparison of Latin America and East Asia". In *Changes in Exchange Rates in Rapidly Developing Countries: Theory, Practice, and Policy Issues*, T. Ito & A. Krueger (eds), 133–54. Chicago, IL: University of Chicago Press.

Sachs, J. & A. Warner 1995. "Natural Resource Abundance and Economic Growth", Working Paper 5398. Cambridge, MA: National Bureau of Economic Research.

Sachs, J. & A. Warner 1999a. "Natural Resource Intensity and Economic Growth". In *Development Policies in Natural Resource Economies*, J. Mayer, B. Chambers & A. Farooq (eds), 13–38. Cheltenham: Edward Elgar.

Sachs, J. & A. Warner 1999b. "The Big Push, Natural Resource Booms and Growth". *Journal of Development Economics* 59 (1): 43–76.

Sachs, J. & A. Warner 2001. "The Curse of Natural Resources". *European Economic Review* 45 (4/6): 827–38.

Salisu, M. 2000. "Corruption in Nigeria", Working Paper 2000/06. Lancaster: Lancaster University Management School.

Sarmidi, T., S. Law & Y. Jafari 2014. "Resource Curse: New Evidence on the Role of Institutions". *International Economic Journal* 28 (1): 191–206.

Schmidt-Hebbel, K. 2012. "Fiscal Institutions in Resource-Rich Economies: Lessons from Chile and Norway", Working Paper 682. Cairo: Economic Research Forum. Available at: http://erf.org.eg/publications/fiscal-institutions-resource-rich-economies-lessons-chile-norway (accessed 30 July 2018).

Shell, K. 1966. "Towards a Theory of Inventive Activity and Capital Accumulation". *American Economic Review* 56 (1/2): 62–8.

Singer, H. 1950. "The Distribution of Gains between Borrowing and Investing Nations". *American Economic Review* 40 (2): 473–85.

Skaperdas, S. 1992. "Cooperation, Conflict and Power in the Absence of Property Rights". *American Economic Review* 82 (5): 720–39.

Skaperdas, S. 2002. "Warlord Competition". *Journal of Peace Research* 39 (4): 435–46.

Smith, A. 1976 [1776]. *An Inquiry into the Nature and Causes of the Wealth of Nations*. Oxford: Clarendon Press.

Smith, A. 2008. "The Perils of Unearned Income". *Journal of Politics* 70 (3): 780–93.

Smith, B. 2004. "Oil Wealth and Regime Survival in the Developing World, 1960–1999". *American Journal of Political Science* 48 (2): 232–46.

Smith, B. 2015. "The Resource Curse Exorcised: Evidence from a Panel of Countries". *Journal of Development Economics* 116 (C): 57–73.

Snyder, R. & R. Bhavnani 2005. "Diamonds, Blood and Taxes: A Revenue-Centered Framework for Explaining Political Order". *Journal of Conflict Resolution* 49 (4): 563–97.

Sokoloff, K. & S. Engerman 2000. "Institutions, Factor Endowments, and Paths of Development in the New World". *Journal of Economic Perspectives* 14 (3): 217–32.

Solow, R. 1956. "A Contribution to the Theory of Economic Growth". *Quarterly Journal of Economics* 70 (1): 65–94.

Solow, R. 1974. "Intergenerational Equity and Exhaustible Resources". *Review of Economic Studies* 41 (5): 29–45.

Stewart, F. 2000. "Crisis Prevention: Tackling Horizontal Inequalities". *Oxford Development Studies* 28 (3): 245–62.

Stijns, J.-P. 2006. "Natural Resource Abundance and Human Capital Accumulation". *World Development* 34 (6): 1060–83.

Sugawara, N. 2014. "From Volatility to Stability in Expenditure: Stabilization Funds in Resource-Rich Countries", Working Paper 14/43. Washington, DC: International Monetary Fund.

Tadjoeddin, M. 2014. *Explaining Collective Violence in Contemporary Indonesia: From Conflict to Cooperation*. Basingstoke: Palgrave Macmillan.

Tilly, C. 1978. *From Mobilization to Revolution*. Reading, MA: Addison-Wesley.

Tilly, C. 1998. *Durable Inequality*. Berkeley, CA: University of California Press.

Timmer, M., G. de Vries & K. de Vries 2014. "Patterns of Structural Change in Developing Countries", Research Memorandum 149. Groningen: University of Groningen, Groningen Growth and Development Centre.

Toscani, F. 2017. "The Impact of Natural Resource Discoveries in Latin America and the Caribbean: A Closer Look at the Case of Bolivia", Working Paper 17/27. Washington, DC: International Monetary Fund.

Torvik, R. 2001. "Learning by Doing and the Dutch Disease". *European Economic Review* 45 (2): 285–306.

Torvik, R. 2002. "Natural Resources, Rent Seeking and Welfare". *Journal of Development Economics* 67 (2): 455–70.

Torvik, R. 2009. "Why Do Some Resource Abundant Countries Succeed While Others Do Not?". *Oxford Review of Economic Policy* 25 (2): 241–56.

Tsani, S. 2015. "On the Relationship between Resource Funds, Governance and Institutions: Evidence from Quantile Regression Analysis". *Resources Policy* 44: 94–111.

Tsui, K. 2011. "More Oil, Less Democracy: Evidence from Worldwide Crude Oil Discoveries". *Economic Journal* 21 (551): 89–115.

Tullock, G. 1967. "The Welfare Costs of Tariffs, Monopolies and Theft". *Western Economic Journal* 5 (3): 224–32.

UNDP1996. *Human Development Report 1996*. New York: Oxford University Press.

Van der Ploeg, F. & S. Poelhekke 2009. "Volatility and the Natural Resource Curse". *Oxford Economic Papers* 61 (4): 727–60.

Van der Ploeg, F. & S. Poelhekke 2010. "The Pungent Smell of 'Red Herrings': Subsoil Assets, Rents, Volatility and the Resource Curse". *Journal of Environmental Economics Management* 60 (1): 44–55.

Van der Ploeg, F. & S. Poelhekke 2017. "The Impact of Natural Resources: Survey of Recent Quantitative Evidence". *Journal of Development Studies* 53 (2): 205–16.

Van der Ploeg, F. & A. Venables 2011. "Harnessing Windfall Revenues: Optimal Policies for Resource-Rich Developing Economies". *Economic Journal* 21 (551): 1–30.

Venables, A. 2016. "Using Natural Resources for Development: Why Has It Proven So Difficult?". *Journal of Economic Perspectives* 30 (1): 161–84.

Venables, A. & S. Wills 2016. "Resource Funds: Stabilising, Parking and Inter-Generational Transfer". *Journal of African Economies* 25 (AERC Supplement 2): 20–40.

Vicente, P. 2010. "Does Oil Corrupt? Evidence from a Natural Experiment in West Africa". *Journal of Development Economics* 92 (1): 28–38.

Voors, M., P. Van Der Windt, K. Papaioannou & E. Bulte 2017. "Resources and Governance in Sierra Leone's Civil War". *Journal of Development Studies* 53 (2): 278–94.

Wacziarg, R. 2012. "The First Law of Petropolitics". *Economica* 79 (316): 641–57.

Weber, M. 2010 [1905]. *The Protestant Ethic and the Spirit of Capitalism*. New York: Oxford University Press.

Wick, K. & E. Bulte 2006. "Contesting Resources: Rent Seeking, Conflict and the Natural Resource Curse". *Public Choice* 128 (3/4): 457–76.

Williams, A. 2011. "Shining a Light on the Resource Curse: An Empirical Analysis of the Relationship between Natural Resources, Transparency and Economic Growth". *World Development* 39 (4): 490–505.

Williams, A. & P. Le Billon (eds) 2017. *Corruption, Natural Resources and Development: From Resource Curse to Political Ecology*. Cheltenham: Edward Elgar.

Wills, S., L. Senbet & W. Simbanegavi 2016. "Sovereign Wealth Funds and Natural Resource Management in Africa". *Journal of African Economies* 25 (AERC Supplement 2): 3–19.

World Bank 2015. *Global Economic Prospects, January 2015: Having Fiscal Space and Using It*. Washington, DC: World Bank. Available at: www.worldbank.org/content/dam/Worldbank/GEP/GEP2015a/pdfs/GEP15a_web_full.pdf (accessed 16 April 2015).

Yusof, Z. 2011. "The Developmental State: Malaysia". In *Plundered Nations? Successes and Failures in Natural Resource Extraction*, P. Collier & T. Venables (eds), 188–230. Basingstoke: Palgrave Macmillan.

Zainal Abidin, M. 2001. "Competitive Industrialization with Natural Resource Abundance: Malaysia". In *Resource Abundance and Economic Development*, R. Auty (ed.), 147–64. Oxford: Oxford University Press.

Zhang, X., L. Xing, S. Fan & X. Luo 2007. "Resource Abundance and Regional Development in China", Discussion Paper 00713. Washington, DC: International Food Policy Research Institute.

Index